A Solitary Traveller

A Solitary Traveller

Svāmi Sadānanda Sarasvatī

Luminary Publications

Luminary Publications
UCYL, Abhedashram, Marcella, Salop Road,
Welshpool, Powys SY21 7ET Great Britain.

First published in the Netherlands by Stichting Luminary
Publications, September 1976.
First published in Great Britain by Luminary Publications. Revised
edition 1995.

ISBN 0 9520522 1 0

PUBLISHERS NOTE

A SOLITARY TRAVELLER is a highly poetical and deeply philosophical work which deals with the life and practices of a sannyasin in the Himalayas.

A SOLITARY TRAVELLER shows the heights and depths of the subject matter and with its natural flow of style it presents many intrinsic and philosophical views alongside the topics of daily life.

Though the author was unable to complete the work to its planned length, the publishers feel that the text in its present form would be of great interest, delight and benefit to all.

The publishers express their gratitude and appreciation to the author for this invaluable text and apologize for any mistakes unwittingly committed by the publishers.

Abhedashram December 1995

Svāmi Sadānanda Sarasvatī

Svāmi Sadānanda Sarasvatī was a Vedantin of high calibre and belonged to the lineage of the illustrious Bhagavatpada (popularly known as Adi Shankaracharya). Svami Sadanandaji was an eminent scholar, poet and Yogi, initiated into sannyasa by Shrimat Paramahamsa Parivrajakacharya Svami Shankarananda Sarasvati.

Svamiji practised rigorous austerities in the Himalayas and a very small part of this time is beautifully reflected in the present work. After his sojourn in the Himalayas Svamiji travelled throughout India, Europe and America benefiting many wherever he went until his mahasamadhi in October 1983. His profound philosophical insight became apparent in his teachings, articles and commentaries on the Yoga sutras, Bhagavad Gita, Vedantasara and other texts.

Widely known for his in-depth knowledge of the mundane and the divine, Svamiji would define objects and concepts with a rare scientific precision. In the present text we find his qualities as a writer, poet, philosopher and saint flowing together on the currents of his innate wit and humour, his lovingness and care for his fellow beings, all washed and refined by the depth of his renunciation and discerning intelligence and wisdom.

Svāmi Sadānanda Sarasvatī in the Himalayas

CONTENTS

Towards Hardvar

It was a long journey! An inspiring and perspiring endeavour! An ascending and descending exercise! I went on walking all the way, in length and breadth. The ascending and descending process of walking continued. Many months had passed on the mountain valley. The majestic snow-clad peaks of the Himalayas and its valleys remained everywhere the same. It had no past nor future; it was present everywhere. But during my sojourn I felt that every step in front of me was a step into the future and every step behind, the past, and my present existed as transitory as possible.

I contemplated! All the day travelling, seeing the Himalayas everywhere present. It has no past but just the present, while I have a past, present and future. Is it not because I think of different objects and because the mind projects the past, present and future, blocking the continuous presence of the present. Is it not because the vast present cannot be perceived by the eyes and because the mind, which has millions of impressions of the gross objects, within, produces the past, future and present in relation to these objects. What in fact is memory? Is it not the presence of the present impression of the object? Is it not the unfoldment of the same folding, just like the unfolding of a big yarn of cloth. If no other impression is carried, except one, how can there be a past and future and a present!

The Himalayas, the king of the mountains! It has many things to tell us. I felt, sometimes it teaches endurance, patience, tolerance and also, I felt, it teaches timelessness. It is a deep philosophy. Perhaps in its unique growth upward, while leaving its height to kiss the heavens, there is something which the mind and senses cannot perceive. It is wonderful! And someone walks! There are many caves, the gateways to its inner mind, but very few know how to get into it. The cave! The density of darkness! It remains in its own self. I was told that many saints were meditating there. It is fantastic and wonderful. The white snow, the melting snow, the dripping snow, the grey snow, the snow all white and the water of no colour. The snow! The Almighty has kept the snow as a transcendental treatment to prevent a chronic burning sensation in its celestial height.

It is interesting to go into the cave! The dripping water! The dripping snow provides a slippery walk inside. It is very easy to lose oneself if one simply enters. Meditation within, is of course, inspiring but meditation within the cave is suffocating, frightening, not only due to its solitude and darkness, but also due to its depth. Perhaps the mountain has its mind in its depth. It may look terrible because the mind, for everyone and of everyone, is always fearsome, dubious and diabolical. Very seldom there is something delightful in the mind.

There are birds, like saints, sitting and singing on the twigs of the trees of fallen leaves. Seldom they sit for meditation but are ever active in playing and crying, in singing songs and quarrelling among themselves. They too attain *samadhi*, in the night, if sleep can be called so - I don't know. But the saints and sages in the caves definitely knew about it. One day I heard that they talked about *Atman* - the attributeless, the omnipresent, the all-divine, the all-knowing, the all-pervading, the all-blissful, the all-existing. I thought, "It is true, because such qualifications alone can exist without any support." It was very interesting to listen how the saints were talking. They talked about the mind as sometimes a projective or a provocative agent - ever doubtful, ever fickle, never settled. It all sounded fantastic, sometimes incomprehensible. But they do talk. If they both knew what they were talking about, why should they then talk at all? Perhaps, knowledge like a river must flow.

There was a small river nearby, just on top of the mountain. It was very fascinating. Within a few minutes it became my intimate friend. It had a style of its own, ever falling down, what you call flowing. It was nice, cool, pure and transparent like a child's smile. It had a spontaneity and continuity ever since it did spring; it never stops. I am sure that it cannot have a past or a future, just like the mountain. It must be present everywhere at the same time. Whenever I felt tired I used to drink a little water from the river and my thirst was quenched; I felt fresh. I always used to think that it is the same with knowledge too! When one obtains knowledge, one is also free from tiredness and weariness, one is happy. Knowledge has no past, no future; it is ever present.

In a long sojourn along the bank of the river, from the top to the bottom, the river is present everywhere; its dancing ripples, its melodious sound, majestic flow, pompous appearance, it is so deep in some places, like knowledge. All are frightened to go there. The past, present and future, as in this mountain and river, I think, do not exist in knowledge. The mountain is so high, the river is so deep; between the two the I, the conditioned, exists.

Quaking fear! Really, it is frightening to be frightened. In the conditioned existence everything is possible. Except one thing, to remain unconditioned. The bliss, happiness and knowledge, all is possible. I heard it from the murmuring of the river, by repeating the sacred syllable *OM*.

In solitude alone, in an unpolluted atmosphere, where there will be no nuisance and menace of the so called good and bad people, contemplation is good. It is good for those who want to contemplate. Wine is good for those who want to be intoxicated. Divinity is good for those who want to be divine. But what one really wants, one very seldom knows. To know what we want, that is knowledge; that is rare. So my sojourn continued.

The hutment! where oil-lamps are burning, even during the day, and where the people who move about are simple and noble, unknown to modern civilisation. They are uncivilised, for frauds and forgery, lies and falsehood, stealing and accumulation, science and technology are unknown to them. A flying aeroplane! It is roaring; they think that the gods are moving with anger.

The cowherds! They move with the cattle, holding a stick. This stick, straight and unbending, when it is used for punishment it is painful. The animals are to be controlled by stick and sound. The cowherds make peculiar sounds to direct the animals. The cattle like the ego go everywhere, no discipline. Like the *guru* and the *mantra*, the stick and the sound control the animals.

They are so compassionate, so hospitable. They offered me milk when they saw me walking as if swinging. They thought that I was tired and hungry. "They are good and nice persons", I thought. Generally, the good and bad depend upon one's own interest. I thought, "If they don't give me milk will I think that they are good?" All want to be favoured.

I went on; felt tired; in meditation, unlike modern meditation, sitting on chairs with shoes on, a fastened tie hanging below the neck, wearing spectacles but keeping their eyes closed. They sit tight for sometime, just emptying the mind. Of course, in modern meditation the privileged ones are the chairs. They are benefited - they have a shift, a lift from theatre to meditation hall.

The small huts are painted tawny; the leaves, the murmuring leaves, change their colours; the white day becomes a golden day; on the sheep and cattle some lovely paintings are sprinkled. The snow-clad mountain-peak shines in golden glittering. Slowly, the end of the day comes; the sun sets. Like great men, like great saints, like great souls, illuminating all within. Only the fools and criminals remain in darkness. In the brilliance of the sun there are places in the mountain where the sun cannot enter. And among the wise audiences there used to be a Judas where the *guru's* advice could not enter.

All is dark. The night, the thick night, the night of twinkling stars and shining moon; no birds sing, no animals move, all were asleep except man. Man is not like animals. He thinks, his mind wanders, his body moves, even in the midnight in solitude when the earth is silent, the mountains are silent, the animals are silent, the birds are silent and the sun is asleep. But man moves: he has a mind; he has intelligence too, but he uses it very rarely, as if he fears lest it will be lost. It was nice to walk, but for how long? Unlike the modern walkers I am to walk, no money, no sleep and no rest.

I walked on into the midnight! The trees meditate! The creepers meditate! The flowers meditate! I was moving! The stars, the crescent moon, up above the sky. The blue sky; they guarded me, as if. A saint was sitting straight erect with head, neck and body. I looked at him. I felt he commands me to sit: I sat.

At dawn my eyes were opened. "You were meditating", said the saint. He told me about meditation, about life, about *Atman*, about the world, about the transcendental and the transient. He explained the *Yoga* and *Vedanta* to me there where I needed coaching. It is true, when one has a burning desire, it is fulfilled. The saint disappeared!

Again the sun was shining. Within me, someone shines. No darkness inside or outside; but the skin, like an idiot, never changes its colour, even when illuminated. Perhaps such is the stuff of its origin - it is destined to be destroyed. What is not self-luminous is a compound product, bound to perish. Anything which is produced cannot shine by itself; that is the wisdom. In the sunlight of the day, I continued my sojourn.

The Himalayas - the abode of snow and gods. It is inspiring to be there, contemplating on the thousands of events that took place in the Himalayas. An eventful mountain. It has an epoch making history. It is an object for poets, for their imagination. Poets try to understand it by imagination; physicians try to understand it through its herbs; botanists try to understand it through analysing the plants; geologists try to measure its age by its stones and earth. They all have their own conclusions and they are satisfied, but the Himalayas remains unexplained. Kalidasa wrote, "Its very soul is God." Thinking of what others have said about it and looking at it again and again, one realises that there is a beauty of the highest magnitude, that there is something most attractive in its altitude and latitude. Still, there is something even deeper. I must say in brief that the *Himavan* is ineffable - a wonderful manifestation in God's creation; an accomplished beauty, grandeur and splendour!

I sat there! I sat there for meditation; it was an ideal place. A lovely valley, eight thousand feet high, full of bushes and grass, trees, creepers and the blue sky above. Occasionally rocking racks and the smiling sun - just contemplating to set for its evening bath in the ocean. The sun, since it has illuminated many sins, needs a bath.

There was a solemn tranquillity, a solitude. The music of the birds and the frequent motion of the animals exercising, their olympic sport rehearsals, some distant sounds of certain animals - sometimes like roaring, sometimes like barking - but they did not disturb me; I love to call it solitude and quietude. That outside world was one with me. I felt they suggested that I should meditate. It was a coincidence: I was about to meditate. And I commenced my contemplation. I sat in lotus-posture on the green grass of even surface.

The *pranayama* - the controlling of the breath - the cosmic air from outside the body; it is drawn slowly and steadily and remains retained for sometime within, as if the breath lost its way out. Like water flows out of an earthen pot, so slowly all what is retained is going out. I felt quite comfortable; I felt the whole universe enter into me through my nostrils. I continued the *pranayama* as an automatic result. No *Himavan*! No sky! No smiling sun! No sound of the birds! No blowing of the wind! I am far away from them; they cannot touch me; I am so far-far off from them! I am already inside.

I felt what is inside. Why should I come inside? I was eager to know. Whom should I ask? My mind was no longer prepared to go out. It rested as if gratified. I went on. I started to think and my intelligence was of course the only one that could help me in this state. I went on repeating the *mantra* and went on contemplating on its meaning. Then the whole attention went towards the point within; that point which is neither black nor white. It is of no substance and yet it is "something". I have found that nothing else exists other than this "something". I was happy and delightful! I went on for a few days.

The hunger and thirst and the other necessities of life came to me like guests, occasionally. There were roots, very sweet and delicate, white and full of milk. One big root was enough for two days. They were around me. I just picked them up. The soil was very soft and fertile, like a mother's heart. It was very easy to uproot them. Together with some *pranayamas* of the *hatha-yoga* they were quite enough to meet the necessities of life.

There was cold, damned cold. It always came in the evenings and went away in the mornings after sunrise. The heat and cold dwelt around me just like persons who are interested in character assassination will sit around the great men. But the great men are not troubled and those persons lose the chance to learn wisdom. It is the same with the heat and cold; they are a luxurious variety of nature, lavishly thrown out like the wealth of a sensual person, in and out of season. But it did not disturb me much.

There was firewood: the dried fallen twigs of the trees - I burnt them. Sometimes, just like the sun, the fire also fears the cold. The fire and the sun, the day and the night, provided a good atmosphere for meditation. I felt that my body was being roasted day and night. I concentrated. The more I concentrated, the more I felt becoming lighter and lighter and my weight became reduced. My object of concentration became more and more clear to me. It had never been so clear before as it was now. I went on.

The intelligence! Ignited by the meaning of the *mantra*, it was passing through and evolving around impressions. It is very difficult to take the intelligence off the impressions; they are like flies. It learned to discriminate between the impressions of the objects. The impressions, like sin-collectors, never vanish, but the intelligence was moving around with the power of the *mantra* in search of something unrevealed just like a small light passing through dense darkness in the night. There is a light which is different from darkness, yet it is in the darkness. The intelligence, with the power of the *mantra*, is carrying the light through the sin collectors - the impressions. It was a new experience.

To disconnect the one impression from the other is very difficult just like the bubbles on foam; they appear and disappear frequently in an unimaginable speed. That gives a restlessness. But the *mantra* is very powerful; it is more powerful than the intelligence itself. Once one is able to have the intelligence to hold the *mantra*, it will never give up. The sound of the *mantra* penetrates into the intelligence, activating it, making it to move within its meaning and sound. This went on for many days.

At last, the intelligence was able, after all it is the intelligence, to discover the vast space where no impressions are stored. The moment it discovers the space, the restlessness ceases; its contact with the impressions has ceased. There was a sigh of relief. It was almost like a man seeing the light and blue sky after walking for hours together through the dense darkness of the woods. There was a stillness, there was a tranquillity, there was a quietude, a blissful achievement. The tired and weary intelligence became refreshed, rejuvenated. Though it was solemnly calm, it regained its nature of discrimination. I never could imagine the meaning of discrimination and determination ever before. The intelligence is so powerful, especially when it is armed with the *mantra*. The space within appeared to be so vast: a cosmic vastness.

I spent many days during my sojourn in this state. A state of intoxication! A realm without any reagent[1] and without being subject to any reagent. A state of consciousness where unconscious-consciousness does not exist and the mind, as it is defined, does not exist. The intelligence becomes conscious. The mountain and valleys, the bushes and trees, the cattle and the cowherds, all remained a conscious continuum. Though the eyes were seeing the gross forms -

---

1. reactive force

the gross manifestations - they were incapable of carrying any impression. A state where it became difficult to determine the visible world, existing within or without me! Any object that is seen through the intelligence is not the object as is seen before, but a conscious continuum. It did not last long, but the bliss continued.

The Himalayas! I thought, the abode of saints and savants, *rishis* and *maharishis*. Their thought-vibrations exist there everywhere. Perhaps, that may also be the reason why the Himalayas became the ideal place for meditation, besides its accomplished climate and natural tranquillity. The silver clouds just float in the air, like children swinging in the cradle. They assume different forms before vanishing, like imaginations or reminiscences of the sweet events of the past. The whispering trees, the blowing woods, the singing bamboos, the fragrant *devadaru* trees, the sporting birds, the running deer, all are peaceful and blissful.

There were small huts beside the caves. Wise men of lore, practising austerities conducive to self-realisation, dwelt there. I just moved on. I sat near a hut. My body felt tired, refused to move, but I was blissful. I had no needs! I was peaceful; I had no desires. I realised that I exist, that I exist within the body, that I will continue to exist without the body. But very often that state of consciousness did not stand continuously. Very often the mind would become active and identify with the body, bringing contradictory experiences: a sadness outside and a helplessness within. Like hungry children eat sweets while crying for their missing mother. I sat there.

A saint came to me. He looked at me, top to bottom. He did not utter a word. He looked at me, as if I was there as an object of his concentration. After a while he asked me to practise *hatha-yoga* postures. He said, "The body is needy, it should be looked after. Every object has its own method of care: the body needs food and certain postures." I practised under his guidance. My body became light and free from sweating, and my mind became calm. I realised that by constant practice of the *hatha-yoga* one can make the body free from ailments and fatigue, maintaining the body with little food. Under his guidance I learned some new techniques of *hatha-yoga* and *mudras* which could keep me smart and active, free from fatigue and lassitude.

The saint! He invited me to his hut. He told me, "There are some night-flies. They are poisonous. They will bite and poison the blood. They sleep in the day and fly in the night. It's better to be in the hut in the night." There was a small lamp - an oil-lamp. He had collected some firewood, but it was not firewood, it was lamp-wood. In the night's darkness one can light it; it will burn for a long time and with a stick of one meter, lit, one can walk a mile in the night. It had a fine fragrance. It is an oily wood.

We both sat there. We ate some roots and drank some water. Cold water; it cools not only the body but also the mind. We went on talking until midnight. We talked about various topics, mainly about the methods of bringing the body under control and the necessity to practise those methods for spiritual attainment. He taught me certain *mudras* which I could not find in any books on *Yoga*. When I asked him, "Have they been written in any books?" he simply laughed. "From books you get milk but from tradition you get butter. I learned them from my *guru*. His words and my experiences are my authority. How did you find them?" he asked. My experience is not different from his. It was easy for me, later on, to move alone, in solitude; it was wonderful. The saint talked to me about introspection.

Introspection! It is a great source of knowledge. It is a fountain of strength and courage. It has a value for spiritual and material life. In the sphere of introspection many experiences occur. I narrated my experiences to him; how I felt the unconscious wakeful state and how I became conscious of it. When I experienced this state as being conscious of an unconscious state, a kind of intoxication, he smiled. He said, "I too had the same. It was thirty years ago. I am here since forty years." He started to tell me of his experiences.

He said, "There are moments during spiritual practices which are frightening at times. They are frightening because the practitioner feels he will lose the world in which he was living, and the memories of the past seem as if they are being lost. Sometimes it is confusing. The confusion comes because of lack of purity of the discriminative faculty. You should know, that when the intelligence depends upon the impressions carried by the mind for its discrimination of the present spiritual experiences that in that state confusion comes and, sometimes, contradiction; contradiction in the context of the comparison of experiences within and the experiences without. It happens because it compares the introspective experiences with the experiences of the external. This is because of a lack of understanding. For example, I have experiences that while I go deeper into contemplation on the Self, my body becomes foreign and the very consciousness of the body is different. I do possess the previous knowledge of the "I" in which the body is included, but now the experience within is that the body is not included in the "I". The body-consciousness slowly vanishes as the concentration becomes more and more pointed, like the disappearance of bubbles on the water. In the tranquillity of the mind - in the introspective state of mind - the "I" has no contact with the body. It was my first experience. Later on, as I continued to have the same state for a long time, I found the whole phenomenal universe like a husk, and a substance within. My consciousness becomes conscious by being present in that substance, and much later I found that the very substance exists in the husk also. Now I do not feel anything other than my consciousness in everything. I see the object, but my understanding is different. I know my body and I use this body like any other tool with a certain purpose. I maintain it as I maintain my clothes and hut", he concluded.

He asked me, "What do you mean by conscious-unconsciousness?" "I mean the wakeful state, that what is called the conscious plane but what is in fact an unconscious plane. The perceiver is not conscious of the reality in the object. He perceives only the surface, without substance. And then he says, "I am conscious of the experience". In fact, that consciousness is unconsciousness, yet there is a consciousness in it. There can be no unconsciousness without consciousness. Therefore I call it conscious-unconsciousness", I replied.

The consciousness! Is it a word denoting an object? Consciousness! Does it have a meaning by itself? Or does it mean something through something? The consciousness! It is a thing in itself! It is a thing in everything, a thing by which a thing can be known, by which a thing can exist as a thing and by which one can know a thing. The consciousness is, in fact, the conscience - the knowledge itself; it exists in the knower, in the known, in the method of knowing and in-between them.

The *sannyasin*! He asked, "Could you explain the philosophy in it?" "The consciousness, like light in the darkness, is present in the unconsciousness. Unconscious-consciousness is that consciousness which is present in unconsciousness. In true psychology the consciousness itself is the psyche", I replied. He said, "It is all right. One can remain conscious only when one becomes consciousness itself. Until then, in fact, one way or the other, all are unconscious."

The consciousness! The consciousness is of two kinds, one is associated consciousness, the other is consciousness itself. Whenever one hears the word consciousness, one thinks of something one is conscious of, but one never thinks, "What is this consciousness?" The true consciousness is the Self itself; it is the existence-knowledge-bliss in its absolute entirety. This consciousness is realised when one finds the consciousness of objects withdrawn into the consciousness itself, by the consciousness, and remaining as consciousness. The associated consciousness is, in fact, the unconscious-consciousness, like light in darkness. There is no darkness without light, but there is light without darkness. Thus the unconscious-consciousness. There is no unconsciousness without consciousness, but there is consciousness without unconsciousness. It is very difficult and also equally easy to understand.

We both slept! We have slept well. In the solitude, in the deep night, within the hut, under the blanket, we heard a penetrating sound. A sound in the wilderness. From where does it come? Where does it go? Why does it come? How a sleeping man can know it! Like a mother's lullaby, that melodious sound added to the sweetness and glory of the sleep. In fact, sleep is very sweet. Deep sleep is deep sweet!

The next day we got up, a bit late, the sun was a bit late to rise. There was damn cold. There was a lovely blanket of fog. When we were out of bed and had just peeped outside, we were playing guitar with our teeth. The *sannyasin*, the experienced soul in the Himalayas, lit his oven and was ready with hot water.

The hot water! In the Himalayas! In an atmosphere of cold war, hot is a genuine weapon. The singing teeth appreciated the warm water, no resistance. The morning duty was over. "Tea is ready", *Svamiji* said. It was a wonderful tea, very fine. I took it.

The tea! The Himalayan tea! It was wonderful. It had a fragrance and a flavour of its own. A prickling taste. It was very pleasant to drink it there. Whether one can appreciate it elsewhere, I don't know. A breakfast followed, made of what? Some roots and some leaves, without salt, as if it was a prescription from a cruel doctor. Tea without sugar and breakfast without salt. What was the greatness and attraction in them? There were two things that made them great. One was, they were hot. Secondly, they quenched the hunger and thirst. That is all. In fact, it was not tea, it was a medicinal herb, rejuvenating!

I continued my sojourn. Farther and farther! I followed the Himalayas, the majestic mountains. Every moment something of the Himalayas pops into my mind. Lord Shiva of Kailasa, Girija of Gowrishringa, Shiva's contemplation, Parvati's[1] practice of austerities to realise Shiva, the Lord of all Lords, the absolute Lord, the Lord associated with pure *sattvaguna* which the mind of Parvati personified. She discovered a dedicated husband in him, as if or "being" the pure *sattvaguna* herself. All these are the sweet memories of what I have heard and read.

I sat down. The great Himalayas at my back, the valley below, infinite space before me. I sat and continued my contemplation on the *guru*.

The *guru* - the *Sadguru* - the all-pervading consciousness, the absolute consciousness, the guiding factor in everyone, the ever present reality. The consciousness itself. He is the *guru*; he is called so because he is the dispeller of darkness. He is present in everyone. He is the consciousness in the unconsciousness. He is the guiding factor in everyone's life. I began to concentrate on him as the plenitude of consciousness. It was wonderful. By his grace, by the grace of the *guru*, the mind became introspective and moved fast towards concentration. As in daily life, so in spiritual life, the presence of the *guru* is a living fact. Thus one can understand the principle of the *guru* more and more: he is neither internal nor external; he is without inside and outside; he is consciousness itself. As long as one possesses the

1. Also known as Girija

idea that the *guru* is inside, one should have a *guru* outside in person until one realises that the *guru* is present everywhere and anywhere, in past, present and future, and beyond inside and outside also. It is wrong to think that God will guide everyone because he is inside and that therefore no other *guru* is needed. It is a wrong assumption. One candle-light is needed to light the other, so one *guru* in person is needed to guide the other person to realise the reality. This process will continue. The *guru* is a person without a person; yet he is a person and yet he is not. "My inner voice, my consciousness, consciousness within me", all are nothing but the expressions of one's own ego and an escape from being disciplined and controlled.

The truth needs no witness, because the truth witnesses itself. It is a self-existing reality. All untruth needs a witness. Whatever is witnessed is unreal, but one unreal may become a means to remove another unreal. Like the one dirt needs another dirt to remove the first one. Like the one thorn is needed to remove the thorn which is in the foot; ultimately, both are not needed. The same with the personal *guru*; the *guru* in person is also unreal, like the ignorance in the disciple, but to remove the ignorance in the disciple a *guru* in person is needed. When the ignorance in the disciple is removed the persons of *guru* and disciple vanish.

While contemplating on this subtle most principle, I felt a sensation within. A sensation almost like the touch of a cool breeze when walking in the scorching sun, or like a dip in a river during a scorching summer. This continued for three hours.

I have already awakened to the unreal world. I got up and continued my sojourn.

Travelling! Travelling deprives one of the time for study and introspection. One gets an opportunity to volunteer oneself to be in the clutches of adversities. Every time there is a different atmosphere, inconsistent and ever-changing! Every step forward is something new and strange: new faces, new places, new situations. Before one becomes acquainted with the nature and behaviour of the environment - animate and inanimate - one leaves for another place. Thus is the travelling, from one place to another. A sojourn - a continuous sojourn - makes one tired and fatigued. It is generally said that travelling makes one wise. It is not true. Most certainly, it cannot have been said by a wise man. Neither travelling nor learning make one wise. It is the obedience, strenuous study and practice under a wise preceptor that makes one wise. One's perception of objects depends upon the type of mind one possesses. Different people perceive the same object in different ways, understand and interpret it in different ways. Therefore, it is the mind of the individual which helps to understand things. A thief is a thief, wherever he goes. A wise man is a wise man even in adverse situations.

Introspection! It needs permanence. Consistency is not possible in motion. Self-restraint and self-composition are not possible in changing attitudes and atmospheres. It commands one to be at one place and constant in the practice of introspection. All spiritual *sadhanas* need dwelling in the same place for a long time. Once one has become introspective and has learned the technique of concentration, then the sojourn helps to gather more and more wisdom, as it gives the opportunity to come into contact with the wise men in different places. Thus my constant travelling in the valley of the Himalayas - for months and months - had helped me to meet many wise men.

It so happened, one day, that I met a *sannyasin*, a *yogi* of the highest magnitude. He was the wisdom embodied. His way of sitting was straight, his walking was straight, his lying when asleep was straight and his thinking was straight. There was no confusion and contradiction in his perception and conception, and in his conversation, no conflicts at all. He said to me: "The Himalayas, when I identify myself with the body and try to look at everything through the senses, my mind experiences the external world, the phenomenal universe, different from myself. When I am in introspection, in sublime culmination, I realise I exist. I alone exist, in the Himalayas, in the whole phenomenal universe. A reality that cannot be negated by any state: wakeful, dream and deep-sleep." It was true.

While we were talking, sitting on a rock, on a sunny afternoon, we saw a shepherd coming towards us, leaving his sheep behind. He walked as if lingering. He came to us, prostrated according to the tradition of his clan, and said, "I am dejected, I am tired and I don't want to go further." "Why?" I asked. "Three of my sheep are missing. The owner of the sheep will kill me. He will think that I have sold them. Please protect me!" "Where is the owner of the sheep?" I asked him. "He is far off," the shepherd said, "a three days walk away." I was just thinking how to solve his problem, I thought I could meet the owner and talk to him and get this poor fellow freed from the blame, but the *Svami* interrupted. "Oh, you should know, it is a test for *sannyasins*. Even in the remote Himalayas, even in the caves, the test comes occasionally, like a toothache. One should pass it. It is a test for you which you should pass. You should tell him where his sheep are." It was difficult. Immediately the *Svami* replied, "You go and count your sheep and the missing ones will be there." The shepherd left. He returned to us to say thanks and that his missing sheep were found. I asked *Svamiji*, that great *yogi*, "What have you done, how could you understand it?" "Oh, it is very simple you just apply *samyama*[1] on the object in your mind. I found the three sheep were coming after him very slowly, far behind, which he could not see, though they were with him."

He was a young boy of twenty years. His next question was, that he was in love with a girl and he wanted to marry her. He had left the Kangra-valley a year ago and he would return there after four months. No correspondence between them; they were illiterate. "Do you love her?" I asked. "During all these months, not even once was she out of my mind; that is how I understand the love", he replied. "Yes, you will get married", I replied. The *Svamiji* was laughing. He said, "It is true, he will get married after he returns home."

The night was very pleasant and delightful. I was practising various methods of *Yoga* under his guidance. The whole night in the Himalayas, in that biting cold, in that magnificent solitude, at the foot of that majestic mountain, the moon remained as a solitary witness of our action and inaction.

A small rivulet was flowing nearby. It had a melodious sound as if repeating the *mantra* of immortality. In its continuous flow, there was a calmness and peace. It was in motion, a spontaneous motion - ever fast, very fast. Yet there was a quietude in its motion. I realised, looking at that motion of the rivulet, the secrecy of inaction in action. When I told this to *Svamiji* he replied, "It is wonderful." He said,

---

1. the c-trinity - concentration, contemplation, culmination

"There is a firmness in the silence of the rock; it is a solid conviction and faith embodied. You see, in its firmness, there is an action. The peace and firmness in the action depend upon the detachment from the action. You can find that this exists within this rock. It acts, it blocks, it hurts, it breaks and yet it is firm and silent. It exists, because there is an absolute existence within the existence of the rock, which is peace and which is silence. Thus you find action and inaction prevail in everything and every being. The moment you understand the secrecy of action in inaction and inaction in action, that very moment you become wise."

At dawn, when the sun was about to rise, we had our bath and were ready for our daily meditation. No coffee, no tea, no hut, no blanket to cover. We had both spent the whole night and sat for meditation. It was shivering cold! For how long! Our shivering continued until we attained concentration. The moment we were in contemplation, the heat and cold did not affect us. There were some birds singing hymns in praise of God, I thought. Some birds of golden wings and musical melodies. They sang well. It helped me in my practice of *pranayama*. How did it help? *OOO...MMMM*; this is how those birds of the golden wings sang at dawn. It showed the way to practise inhalation, retention and exhalation. For all *yogic* practices the nature of the Himalayas has a preceptor to offer. Perhaps that is the reason why *sannyasins* always prefer the Himalayas.

Just after the normal meditation I felt hungry but I refused to think of hunger. Since the afternoon of the previous day we had nothing to eat. Normally we ate two or three roots per day. Those roots, however, were not found in that region of the Himalayas. There were some lovely creepers; they had no flowers though their leaves looked like flowers: half white and half green. They had an astringent taste in the beginning but were sweet in the end, like the wise man's words or advice. There was a method of eating them and *Svamiji* was very pleased to teach it to me.

The *sannyasins* in the Himalayas have their own individuality in everything. All their knowledge, as their self-realisation, is traditional and continuous.

I just contemplated on continuing my sojourn when *Svamiji* said, "I will accompany you!"

We walked! The dawn stood attired in a tawny garment dipped in the colouring of the rising sun. It gave a resemblance of the saint's arrival in the house of the Hindus. The morning, in spite of the spraying snow-dew, it smiled! It needed concentration for both of us to walk and see. We walked a long distance, of course; the few months continuous walking had given me the confidence that I could compete with any horse. The walking kept us in motion for a long time, contemplating on the question "Why we should walk? Why we should go? Where to go?" "There is only one reply, in fact, is it not", *Svamiji* said of his own accord. What does it mean of his own accord; accord of whom? Who is it that wants it? The ego, the mind, the senses and the body, whereas I remain a witness, unmoving, like a person sitting in a train: the train moves but the person does not. So the "I" in the body.

We proceeded! On the way we heard a sound. The sound came from a distance like drum beating, singing, dancing - we did not know what it was. But the natural flow of our moving was towards the village from where the sound came. It was almost eleven o'clock. A long walk, a continuous walk.

We entered into a crowd. A girl was sitting in the middle. She was absolutely naked, declaring herself as all-powerful and able to destroy the whole world whenever she wanted, and announcing that she was a goddess. So the people around her in the village worshipped her as a goddess. We were surprised to see this happening and did not understand at first. *Svamiji* said, "It is a disease, we shall cure that disease!" I asked, "How?" He replied, "It will be very quick." So *Svamiji* and myself appeared before her. The moment she saw us she was disinclined to express her claim. She was silent. When we approached, the others said, "Don't go near her, she is a goddess, she will destroy you!" "We are already dead", I replied. Then the girl looked at us; she was very happy to hear that we were dead. *Svamiji* went near her and told her, "If you don't stop this stupid thing, then I will beat you." *Svamiji* repeated this *mantra* three times, "I will beat you." Suddenly she cried for a *sari* to cover her body. Her being a goddess and all her power of destruction and production disappeared. She came into a normal.

Svamiji said to me later on, "You see, these are hallucinations. You can find this even in big cities, generally with girls, when there are many persons around to praise them in all whatever they do! If others say that it is right then it is right, and a little bit of forest-*Vedanta* of "I am *Brahman*, I am God" and thus they start to think in that line and start to perform. When it is done in the presence of others who cannot counteract them, then the hallucinations can grow. It assumes the form of a phobia within, mania outside. The hallucinations, phobia and mania are due to the incapability of disciplining the mind and the senses. Once you are able to discipline the mind and the senses you can get rid of all these conditions. And the same is the case with schizophrenia. This needs a regular disciplining of the mind. The constant practice of *pranayama* and meditation will remove all these."

We left the place and walked a long distance. We set forth on our journey towards Gangotri and Yamunotri. The trodden path - like snakes, curved and long - passed through bushes, green grasses, rocks, trees and in some places through bare land; we had to walk this path for a long time. It was very pleasant to walk through the valleys of the mountain. Its aspiring height, its firmness, its immovableness; it is wonderful! Very often during our walking I pondered over the substratum of this earth and the mountain, over what it is and how it keeps its balance! How such a huge planet can stand in space and how it moves, constantly, all the time! Like the moon and the sun, the earth too stands in space. As water in a pot, the ocean also may be water in an infinitely bigger pot. At the bottom there must earth and thus it prevents the water from falling down. Thus my thinking continued - not on a scientific basis, of course, but a general way of thinking. Whatever may be the scientific explanation, it cannot be the truth itself. Science explains something that is manifested but the cause remains unexplained. And still more obscure is the cause, which is no longer a cause when we come to know what it is. Thus my thinking went on.

After a few hours walking we found a few thatched hovels in which people were living and we went to them for food. They were very generous and kind and before our asking they offered us food and water. They were very simple people. They were very pure, peaceful and happy. They were not spoilt by civilisation and did not know how to speak lies nor did they know how to dishonour and bluff a person.

As the sun was about to set to take its bath in the ocean, we decided to spend the rest of the day with them.

They saw us sitting for meditation. They heard us talking about *samadhi*, *Atman*, mind and so on. Then one of them, with due respect asked us, "What is it that you talk between yourselves? Are you talking about God? If so, I would like to listen. Please, tell us something about God." We were very happy and *Svamiji* told me, "You see, how wonderful they are. They are very happy. They don't have a desire; they are satisfied with what they have; they want to know about God. They can't understand philosophy." *Svamiji* asked him, "What do you know about God? About how it is and what it is? Why do you want to know about God?"

There was a small hut nearby with a small oil-lamp burning inside. Pointing to it he told us, "My God is there; He protects me, my family and my wealth." "What is your wealth?" I asked him. "Oh, that is these thatched hovels, my three cows and a dozen sheep, myself, my children and my wife", he replied. Then I asked him, "How do you know your God protects you?" He said, "Whenever we have any illness, any trouble, we pray to that God and we are relieved and our diseases are cured. Whenever my cows and sheep are missing, we pray to God. Within a short time they come back to me, unhurt, and we get good crops when we pray to God. Thus we understand that our God is very peaceful and protects us." It was a convincing explanation of God. So I asked him, "Have you seen God?" "Oh, yes," he replied, "every day we go there to see Him and pray. He is very kind and compassionate." "Has your God talked to you?" I asked. "No," he replied, "Man talks, God acts. This is how we experience Him." "You are right. Wonderful!" I said. "Why does your God remain inside the hut?" I asked. He replied, "Though God is everywhere, we need a place to feel Him. So there, we feel His presence much more than anywhere else". Though life is everywhere in the body, we feel only through the senses. It is similar. "Yes, let us go and sit there", I told him and *Svamiji*. We all went there and sat.

There was a small stone, besmeared with vermilion all over. The *mandikam*[1]; that is how he called it. The small hut with inside a God

---

1. the temple of God

conceived in a stone! This has its own philosophy and psychology. It is a most scientific truth that concentration on one point in the infinity, anywhere, at any place, on any object, enables to generate and perceive an all-pervading object. Similarly, the frequent movements of the fan produce air, though air is present everywhere; like digging a well to find water, though water is everywhere. Like looking upwards to perceive a blue sky, though sky is everywhere and without colour; like perceiving a wife in a particular girl, though there are many girls; so the infinite, omnipotent, omnipresent, omniscient God is perceived in a stone, in a piece of wood, in reptiles, in animals and in human beings. It was surprising that though the person was illiterate, uneducated, knew nothing about the mind and its power, nor anything about the definition of God or its erudite explanations, yet, he understood the practical approach to it and he felt happy. When we sat in the temple, the small hut where he accommodated the image according to his concept of God, we experienced a peace and a blissful atmosphere. That atmosphere was created by the devotee's pure mind and pure thoughts. According to him he depended upon God for everything. Really, he dedicated everything to God, as if he was a real *karma-yogi*. But he knew nothing about detachment and nothing about the fruits of actions and their renunciation. These, the puzzling psychology and philosophy of *karma*, did not trouble him at all, not even for a moment. He had faith, implicit faith and dedication.

But others who consider themselves civilised, educated, reasonable and rational are subjected to doubts, dubious speculations, irrational rationalism, unscientific science, non-psychological psychology and philosophy without the "sophy". They suffer and create problems, not only for themselves but for others also. Such people, with a lack of faith and knowledge and a lack of the concept of reality, make others' lives also impossible. They are individuals having many unknown individuals in themselves.

After the meditation we had our supper with his family. He had a small family, consisting of his wife and two children, and his mother and father. Without practising birth control he had only two children. All were collectively responsible for their existence; no problem of aged people as they were looked after by their children. A family self-contented: God and themselves, that constituted their family. Even then the intrusion of the government, like illness in a healthy body, came to collect the revenues. That was the only occasion for them to know that there was a government. Similarly, there were a few families staying in the same place but at a little distance. They all assembled together twice a year before the temple. It was their annual festival day.

The next day the sun was a little kind; it was out of its blanket a little earlier. After breakfast we continued our journey towards Gangotri and Yamunotri through Hardvar and Hrishikesh. We did not leave the inspiring majestic mountains, the Himalayas. We just moved on foot through its valleys, leaving behind us many memories of the past. We used to sit together on the way, talking for one or two hours. The rest of the time we spent in contemplation. We used to walk for four hours in the morning and for four hours in the evening. We never felt any fatigue or tiredness. We followed the pathway trodden by the cattle, cowboys and shepherds. It was a very beautiful sight: it would sometimes shine in the middle of green meadows, like the parting of the hair, and in some places it appeared like a long snake. It was very beautiful to see, very lovely to imagine. The sun was very happy; it went on smiling, sometimes laughing, very seldom the mind of the atmosphere was clouded. Occasionally a reminiscence of the past came to us, such as the memory of certain *yoga* practices when we needed them. We proceeded on our journey smoothly, uninterruptedly.

A long walk! Ever since man learned to walk he never ceased. Death alone is capable of stopping him from walking. Why does he walk? Can a man live without walking? Is it the mind that prompts one to walk? Then why does a person who obtained victory over the mind and senses walk? If it is the intelligence which prompts one to walk, then why do the persons who obtained the culminent intelligence, *samadhi-prajna*, walk? Then what about if it were the ego? But one who has no ego also walks. Why does one walk? I could not find an answer to this question. When I was among the wise men, I had enough opportunity to put this question, but I did not; it never occurred to me. I concluded for myself that as all the three *gunas* existed in the body, the *sattvaguna*, though it was predominant, sometimes commanded the *rajoguna* to act. The *sattvaguna* prompted the *rajoguna* for its own perfection. A cloth can be cleaned once it becomes dirty, by undergoing a certain process. Similarly, to keep away from pollution,[1] the *sattvaguna* prompts the rajoguna to perform actions conducive to purification: to meet wise men, to go to centres of learning and to see holy places where heaven and earth meet in its blooming glory. Hence, the wisest amongst men used to walk. This is the only answer I could find, right or wrong. This answer gave me a satisfaction.

We walked! A long distance! Sometimes, as we did not find a direct path to Gangotri through the Himalayan mountain, we had to come down, in some places, and pass through villages not many miles away from the mountain valley. We met, on the way, a few saints, as if lightning appeared. They were brilliant and visible, but some equally invisible as a saint whom we met on the Himalayas and who walked straight. No mountain, no woods, no trees could stand in his way. Wherever we went we would find him sitting. So one day, within three days, I asked him, "How could you walk straight?" He said, "Space is curved; when your mind is straight, space also becomes straight." It was a puzzle to me. I was pondering over it. Anyhow, it gave us a good subject for discussion. We came to the conclusion, that space is the product of the mind or mind-property. Sometimes the wise son controls his mother and father.

We walked through the dense forest. The wild animals, terrifying reptiles, beautiful serpents, love-making snakes, interlocking animals, caressing creepers, meditating vegetation, shining plants and luminous herbs had become subject to our vision, just to steal our mind from God, as if God was hurt by our constant thinking of Him. After many weeks walking, though we never felt tired, but as a matter of fashion, we took rest. It was very near to Hardvar, only hundred miles away. Our contemplation towards Gangotri was that much near. There were no huts nearby, no human population. We had no problem of starvation as we did not have time to think of food. The dwelling hunger within could not come to us, as a newly wedded girl waiting for a chance to meet her counterpart who is engaged in meditation. The moment our thoughts were disconnected from God, that very moment

---

1. like lethargy

the hunger caught our neck and we felt all the hunger and tiredness in the world fall upon us. Since the last three days we never knew such things ever existed. The other *Svamiji* told us, "It is because the saint whom we met three days ago gave us his blessings." It was so silent, like the wisdom in an idiot or like love in a criminal. Hence we did not know the power of that saint and his blessings. Unless one thinks about all the aspects of a person, one can never understand him. But in general we understand a person only by his expressed aspects.

After a few days walking we reached near Hardvar. We decided to spend a few days in Hardvar and Hrishikesh and then proceed to Gangotri. Thus we changed our direction. It took three and a half days for us to reach Hardvar. When we were walking on the bank of the river Ganga[1] we found many amusing things. Floating stones - stones that float! A hunter told us that you could see the name of Rama on the stones. Therefore they floated! We had never heard before that a stone could float by having letters which read Rama.

It all seemed a wonder! We just went down to the river, took a stone and felt that it was very light, like paper. Of course, the word Rama was written on it in Sanskrit, so we could easily understand that somebody had written that on it. We had seen many other similar stones also in the river Narmada, near Omkareshvar. There, too, the stones were bearing names like Rama, Krishna, Shiva and so on. While we were walking we saw a saint sitting on the bank, writing on such stones. We asked him, "Why do you do it?" He said, "It is my hobby. This is only a pastime for me after the meditation."

We continued walking on the banks along the river Ganga. At times we felt that the Ganga was following us. We put some floating stones on the river, just to follow us, and then walked ahead of them. It took time for the stones, a full one hour, to reach us.

Birds! They, too, were going to Hardvar, as if God had sent them to show us the path. They talked many things between themselves. We interpreted it in our own way, as we wanted. Sometimes, our interpretations were such: "You are tired; the sun is about to set; don't proceed further now; take rest here." Really, we wanted to take rest. The day was becoming dark. The tawny painting of the morning sun

---

1. Ganges

had vanished during the day, and now the setting sun acted as if it was repairing this painting. As if it wanted to keep it safe by covering it with darkness, to be seen again in the morning. We thought, if we walk further in the darkness his paintings may become spoiled. We, too, love his paintings more than our walking; so we stopped.

We could not find any huts nearby to dwell in, so we took shelter under a tree. After some time we felt that it was not good to sleep under the tree, as birds and some animals might have made their homes in the tree. So we shifted to another place where there was a cave. In a cave we had nothing to fear. There might be some snakes, scorpions or spiders, or something similar, but they are not so harmful as some human beings.

The next morning we had our bath and meditation. We were a bit hungry and thirsty but found nothing to eat. We took the Ganga's water. This always increased the appetite while it quenched the thirst. We went on walking, very often drinking water from the Ganga. At twelve o'clock we came across someone with some bread soaked in cooked vegetables, as if waiting for us. The moment he saw us he said, "I have been here since the morning, waiting for you. You are very hungry, eat this!" It was enough for us. We took the bread and the man disappeared. We could not find anyone in the near vicinity. For a hungry man God comes in the form of food, for the thirsty man in the form of water, for the child in the form of the mother, for a woman in the form of her husband.

We had a repose on the smooth back of a huge rock. When we got up we saw two persons standing before us. They were dressed like saints with well-built and tall bodies. I asked them, "Who are you?" and "Where are you going?" They replied, "We are just wandering towards Hardvar." So they followed us. They were closely watching our movements and conversation. When they could not find what they wanted they asked us, "What is your name? Where are you going? Who are you?" These were strange questions to us as these are impossible questions in India to put to *sannyasins*, especially in Hardvar, Hrishikesh and Benares. Naturally we did not take any notice of their questions. Then came the threatening: "If you don't answer our questions you will have to suffer." We replied, "What do you mean by suffer? We know of supper but we never knew what is suffer." Those persons became irritated. We walked on. They stopped us and again started to talk. They repeated the same questions. Then the other *Svamiji* told me, "You see, when a buffalo comes to hit you don't read scriptures to it. A buffalo is a buffalo not a human being. Sometimes we find buffaloes among human beings also." I got the idea. As these persons were talking in English, *Svamiji* wanted me to handle them, as he knew only Sanskrit and Hindi. So I told them, "It is surprising - why do you follow us? And who are you? What do you want?" They refused to answer. Then I said, "Only some criminals and policemen can be such accomplished buffaloes among human beings. And you say that we will have to suffer - without knowing what would become of yourselves! If you don't answer my questions, we shall hand you over to the people not to any police station."

They became angry. We were laughing. The more we laughed the more their anger increased. Their position was very awkward. As we were moving on, we reached some nearby villages. They were frightened. The villagers assembled around us as usual and invited us for supper. It was the first supper after many days. I asked the villagers to question these people and find out who they were: "Don't allow them to go!" When they were encountered by the villagers in their own way, these persons had to reveal themselves as policemen in search of criminals. It was an interested thing. Persons move in this region in search of God, attired in the garment of *sannyasins* and ever in contemplation, ever in conversation on spiritual topics, ever among holy persons. Therefore I asked them: "You are supposed to be the protectors of law and order then why do you violate the social and religious convictions, traditions and ethics? Don't you think this kind of act will create more disbelief in God, religion and spiritual life? Are you not worse than a social criminal? Who authorised you to attire the garments of the *gurus*?" They were silent. We removed their clothes, asked them to wear their own and then sent them back to their own place.

The next day we approached Hardvar. The incident of the previous day was very amusing. We had heard before that these tartarian tribes of the government used to dress like saints and wander about. But we had never come across one before. Hence it was a novel experience. When we were five miles close to Hardvar, we took our bath and sat for meditation. Then we proceeded.

Meditation - dwelling in a world within, concentrating on the impressions or on the space within or directing the mind towards the Self. It is altogether a different world, a world of impressions, of the objects perceived. When we perceive an object outside with the mind through the senses, the object completely vanishes and remains as an impression in the subliminal mind, in the base of the mind, and the outer object, what we say in general "I know this and that", "I know him", is nothing but an impression projected from inside to outside by the mind through the senses. The base of the mind is like a lake. The moment an object disappears in the depth of the lake it remains unseen. Similarly, every object which we perceive and conceive goes deep to the base of the mind and leaves waves caused by the contact with the object outside. Hence we are unable to know the object. We speak in general of these waves, but not of these objects - they remain unknown in us. Thus we have millions of objects stored in the base of the mind. Meditation is the process to know what the object is.

Meditation! A most wonderful and perfect means to know what is within! There is the Self within; there is the base of the mind - the *citta* - within, covering the Self like the thinnest transparent glass placed on the surface of the pure water of the lake. Meditation will reveal the object unknown whether it is inside or outside. In fact, what is inside is also outside. Thus meditation is a wonderful means to reveal the truth within ourselves.

The thing by which the senses are attached to objects is the mind. In fact, it is not the senses which are running after the objects, it is the mind. The mind can perceive several things at the same time, while understanding nothing! It creates conflict and confusion, that is but natural. When one is trying to understand an object, with the mind alone, one understands nothing. But if one can concentrate on the object one tries to understand, it becomes comprehensive. Therefore meditation assumed an importance in the process of comprehending the real nature of an object. The process of comprehension is free! This aspect of comprehension is beyond all apprehension for security and happiness. In right understanding there is no fear. When there is fear there is ignorance. Any action of a man is directed by two factors, the one is ignorance the other knowledge. If one finds fear in any action, one should know that it is ignorance and that has to be eliminated. So meditation is most essential in all human individuals to be able to understand the reality of any object that can be perceived.

The meditation continued for six hours. It was a pleasant day. The time for food was spent in meditation.

The Mind! How it withdrew from the senses! The moment the mind was disconnected from the senses, that very moment the senses returned to their own place, as if they followed their master - the mind. Man has to pass through many brilliant Himalayan passes of all whatever has been heard, seen, conceived and perceived like the concentrated mind has to pass through millions of impressions, like a large fish crosses the turbulent water from one shore to the other, and the mind surrenders to the intelligence like an obedient disciple to the *guru*. The intelligence discriminates what the identification is and then takes an absolutely new form. The discriminating and discerning process is very difficult to explain, but one experiences all this. It is impossible to know the greatness of meditation through scriptures and books. It is to be known from our experience. It is not mere passing through a dark region but it is like passing through a dense wood in the lunar light. It is the consciousness that dispels all the darkness of ignorance and cleanses the sensory nerves etc. Meditation is very simple, at once very difficult, a stupendous endeavour, the most magnificent and majestic indwelling process.

We were about to leave for Hardvar, when a man with his wife appeared, with great devotion, and invited us to spend the rest of our days in his home.

The householders! A house for themselves; they are attached to it. As the ego in the body they dwell there. They have accepted something from this world; that is their only mistake. To maintain and protect what they have accepted, they have to maintain and accept many more things. Thus they construct a world of their own. What they get in return is nothing but a happiness soaked in sorrow. It is like a patient who, while undergoing an operation under the influence of an anaesthetic, is not at all conscious of the cutting of his body; in that state he does not feel what is going on around him; one may call it happiness or whatever one likes. Similarly, householders are unconscious about what is going on around them as a result of the anaesthesia of attachment, produced by ignorance. As long as they remain in that state they are happy, but fortunately, if they happen to become conscious of their plight they realise that they are in the middle of some turbulent water from which it is very difficult to escape. It is then that the search for liberation comes. While drowning in these turbulent waters they need someone to save and protect them. Whatever they thought of as happiness is nothing but misery, just like thinking that one sees water when all it is a mirage. The householders who have awakened from this unconscious state, which they call a conscious state, into the real conscious state, they are in search of the *guru*. They become interested in *Vedanta*.

The householders, the husband and wife, approached us with due reverence and devotion to invite us to spend the rest of the coming days in their home. They were aspirants of *Vedanta*. "We want to know something about ourselves", they asked. "Who is that ourselves who wants to know the ourselves?" I asked.

The ignorant ego very often carried them and seldom gave little chance to hear something beyond itself. And what is that something? The ego reflects the reality when the intelligence is pure - that reality is the absolute in everything. It all sounds somewhat funny. When the ego is predominantly *rajoguna* and *tamoguna* it projects things, it never becomes introspective, it always runs after objects identifying with them and it creates problems. But fortunately, if by chance it becomes predominantly sattvaguna it likes to know about itself and God. It then understands right from wrong. When the ego continues to remain for a long time in a sattvaguna state, only then concentration is possible, only then the mind becomes introspective. It is in this state that one develops a desire to know oneself. In this state one likes to know about meditation and one becomes pure, devoid of projections and associations with mundane objects and thoughts.

This particular family lived nearby at a few miles distance and several great scholars and their two sons accompanied them. There were many persons who had acquired a very good command of *Vedantic* texts and had practised the *yogangas* to a certain extent. The questions were to the point suggesting their answers. They did not disturb us. The *Svamiji* who was with me was fond of speaking very little as he realised the futility of talking too much. What I talked for an hour he could talk the same within five minutes. Hence, the whole responsibility of answering questions rested upon me. The question of initiation came up. Unfortunately, I did not know much about the initiation for such aspirants. I was taught only how to initiate family-people and lifelong celibates and also how to initiate into *sannyasa*.

The family and the audience were between the lifelong celibates and the ordinary householders. We call them aspirants of *vanaprasthashrama*, those setting forth for knowledge. "How can a person living with a wife be initiated into the practice of celibacy and meditation?" they asked. It was a strange question which I had never expected. I just looked at *Svamiji* who was sitting near to me to save me from this confrontation but he was cool to the situation like Himalayan snow. He looked at me and said, "Carry on." I did not know how it happened but by his grace I was spontaneous ever since, up to the present, in answering questions of any type. I explained to them the meaning of celibacy and meditation, and where to meditate. They had the idea that they should meditate on the heart in the chest, or between the eyebrows, or even on some external objects. But when I explained to them that the *hrdaya* mentioned in the texts of the *Upanishads*, *Vedanta*, *Yoga-sutras*, *Yogavasishtha* and others, is not in the chest but in the head, it was a surprise to them. This heart is like a white lotus, which is turned upside down, having its stem upward, penetrating the crown of the head. That is the brain, that is the *hrdaya*. Five fingers from the crown of the head there is a subtle space having the size of the thumb, there resides the Self or soul - the *jiva*. That is the *hrdayakasa*, the space in the *hrdaya*. There one should meditate. This *hrdaya* is also called *shirohrdayam*[1], *samvid-hrdayam*, *upadeya-hrdayam*, *sahasra-padmam*[2], *Brahmapuri*[3]; these are some of its synonyms and the stem is the *sushumna*. The *brahmins* keep their *shikha* exactly above the space in the *hrdaya*. That is the place where one should meditate. It is neither right nor left in the chest.

Having heard this *Svamiji* said, "Exactly true, that is the right

---

1. the heart of the head
2. the thousand petalled lotus
3. the city of *Brahman*

place, that is the place of the *hrdayakasa*." Then those scholars asked me to substantiate my statement. I profusely quoted from the *Upanishads, Yogavasishtha, Bhagavad Gita, Ayurveda, Charaka, Sushruta* and others, and also according to the tradition, the way we practise. They were convinced.

The night went fast, as if frightened of hearing talk on spiritual subjects. All the ignorance within felt tired, it wanted to sleep. When the audience had retired and left us alone *Svamiji* enlightened me on the initiation and after an hour and a half meditation we went to sleep. The next morning, the day of the initiation of the family was very important to me.

Initiation! A turning point in one's life. Initiating into a new life. Initiation! Spiritualising the material life. Balancing its weight. Illuminating the value of life. Focusing on the reality within and without. Elucidating the reality of the perception. Unfolding the futility of mundane living. Expounding the nature of the senses, mind, perception, ego and all internal mechanisms. Imparting the knowledge of the functions of the gross, subtle and causal bodies and the technique of disconnecting these bodies from one another while living in them. Giving light to the technique as how to enter into the subtle body and from the subtle body to the causal body and from the causal body to the Absolute Reality - the Self, while one lives in the conscious-unconscious plane, the wakeful state. Initiation is an illumination of the internal reality. It is a method of unfolding the all-pervading reality. Therefore, initiation is very significant in one's life. Imparting the technique and the *mantra* and other auxiliaries, such as *pranayamas*, might vary according to the individual and their purposes.

It was the rainy season. The morning! Its dawn had a smile as innocent as that of a baby. Some of the trees and plants in the flower-gardens unfolded their flowers, whatever little they had like the little opportunity to be happy for a family-man. The flowers shone in the gardens like the few teeth that appear in the mouth of a child. They made their presence known by their glamour, grace and fragrance. The sky was clear like the mind of a *sannyasin*, a *jnana-yogi*. The clouds had disappeared. There was a stillness which was generally found in the mornings in the villages situated in the mountain-valleys. The birds, of course, were like babies singing their own songs; they would always find an opportunity to express themselves. The torrential rain of the previous night had cleaned the mountains, the trees and all the plants as if they were waiting for initiation with flowers and fruit to offer. Though it was silent there was some noise there to break the sanctity of the silence. There was an instrument which produced a sound, similar to that of the cry of a cur. They call it a harmonica; that horrible musical instrument which is played just to quench the hunger of the music-mania. The neighbouring house was fond of enjoying the non-harmonic sound of the harmonica.

The initiation, it was brooding in my mind. The *pranava*! I was contemplating on it. The *pranava* and its recitation! First one recites this sacred syllable *OM* imagining its meaning, and negating the gross body by concentrating on the consciousness associated with it. Then comes the second stage of the concentration on the *pranava*. While contemplating on its meaning one negates the subtle body by concentrating on the consciousness associated with it. In the third stage the concentration is on the consciousness associated with the causal body, and finally the concentration on the absolute consciousness, the true Self, devoid of all associations. I spent some time in this meditation.

At the appointed time, six o'clock in the morning, the couple came for initiation. It was a new experience for them, for me too! *Svamiji* had explained that the *guru*-disciple relationship is of two kinds. One is beginning from the previous birth, and that alone is successful and permanent. There the *guru* and disciple are devoted, dedicated and faithful to each other. The second is not so. The second variety is plentiful and everywhere; the first one is very rare. After the initiation we had our breakfast and at nine in the morning we left for Hardvar. We walked; the legs were our favourite conveyance. We walked and looked at the vegetation, bushes and trees being the manifestations of the *gunas* on the consciousness, in collaboration with the consciousness present within them. Thus, enjoying the natural scenery, walking slowly and steadily, we reached Hardvar at twelve noon.

A Solitary traveller

The four months stay

Hara Dvar - it means the door to the destruction of all afflictions; this is how people have come to call it. It has a history of many many centuries, surpassing the AD and BC notions of biased historians. This is the place where many saints and sages have practised and are practising austerities and have attained realisation. This whole landscape of the Himalayan valley, stretching many miles, was once forest infested with wild animals; all of this, the forest and the animals, has now disappeared like the ignorance and fickleness of a *yogi*. It is common to many places in India's life that wherever *sannyasins* meditate and live, cities appear later on; even today this is a fact. The modern cities of Benares, Hardvar, Hrishikesh and others are the immortal witnesses to this fact.

In ancient days, as it is today, but it is rare, the householders, *grhasthas*, after their fifties, give up all the responsibilities to their children and retire into seclusion in the forest; some with their wives, some without, and lead the life of a *yogi*. The "*vanaprastha*" means one who has left his home for knowledge. "*Vana*" means knowledge of *Brahman* or the knowledge of plenitude; it has another meaning, i.e. forest. In the latter sense, it means one who left his home for the forest to lead a solitary life, after leading the life of a family man. In both senses the word stands. This is the third stage in the life of a man, to be led according to the law of righteousness of the Hindus.

The *sannyasins* and celibates are all alike leading their life in the forest in contemplation on absolute reality. In former days, unlike today, they used to eat fruit and roots and live ever in contemplation on God, recording their experiences. It was and it is a compulsory custom of tradition that the saints should record their own experiences and revelations on every subject. Some *vanaprasthas* used to do research in the human and animal anatomy and on herbs. Thus many authentic texts were written on the great *Ayurvedic* system, the like of which the world has yet to see. They made their study of anatomy and botany not on dead animals and dried herbs but on living human beings, in fact, in their own body and in the body of living plants by applying c-trinity, *samyama*. The *sannyasins* and some of the *vanaprasthas* recorded their experiences of self-knowledge. It is their recorded experiences and traditionally imparted technique of meditation which are the guiding stars to their austerity. Such brilliant, majestic, accomplished luminaries of Self-knowledge, and of other branches of science, transformed the forest into a seat of knowledge; this attracted the seekers of knowledge to sacrifice their city life and to study, sitting at the feet of the *gurus*.

Hardvar, the modern city, at the foot of the Himalayas shines like a queen among all the cities of the world. It has the glamour and grace of a realised soul, the majestic and dignified appearance of an absolute monarch, the comfort and convenience of a well developed city and at the same time that of a remote, modern village. The Ganga, the holy river of India, flows pompously, purifying and fertilising both banks, producing trees, herbs and all whatever is necessary for animals and super-animals, cultivating saints and sages, savants and *sadhus*. Its transparent water, its majestic flow, its cool breeze, even during winter, produces a profound impact of tranquillity and purity in the minds of those who come into its contact.

The *kumbhamela* takes place once in twelve years, and once in six years the people celebrate the *ardha*[1] *kumbhamela*. Saints, sages, *sadhus* and *sannyasins*, belonging to Shankara's order, and the families from all over the country assemble together; thus it became most important in the life of the nation. Every leaf of a tree, every blade of grass, every grain of sand, every piece of stone, every drop of water, every petal of a flower, every animate and inanimate object has something of meditation and realisation about it; there is something of the *sannyasins*, who are realised and have attained *samadhi*, that is conveyed to the people. Above all, many *sannyasins* are there to study *Vedanta* and *Yoga*. A curious visitor can find that every ashram of *sannyasins*, belonging to Shankara's order. They are the abode of learning the philosophy of *Vedanta* and the abode of practice of what has been learnt. They all look like envelopes enclosing *shravana*, *manana* and *nididhyasana*[2]. The moment the gate of any *sannyasa ashram* is opened, the visitor can find all these three together. There are no *ashrams*, or *sannyasins* in fact, who do not practise all three, every day of their life. They all read and study Sanskrit to know the non-dual reality, mentioned in the *Upanishads*. As the Acharya

---

1. half
2. listening, contemplating and meditating

Shankara has clearly mentioned that this cannot be understood through any native language, or books written about it in any language, but only through the *Upanishads*: *na tu bhasagranthena*[1]!

Thus Hardvar has the privilege, sanctity and credit of a university, imparting the technique and knowledge of the non-dual reality or *Brahman*.

Walking in the morning had almost become our habit. When we came closer and closer to Hardvar, the noise and business of the city life had started to appear. It all looked very strange and unpalatable but we had been able to maintain our peace of mind within ourselves. With our wit and humour and topic of conversation confined to our spiritual practices and to the non-dual reality, the multitude could not influence our solitude.

Hardvar! It has a long association with history as many historical events took place there and this has led it to be known as *itihasa* - "Thus it happened here". More popular among all these events is the story of the nectar-jar. It runs thus. The *devas*[2] and the *asuras*[3] together were in want of an adventurous project. They decided upon producing nectar by churning the ocean. The Mahameru mountain was the churn-staff, and for the churn-rope a large and very long serpent agreed upon this function. While the *asuras* held its forepart the *devas* took its rear. Thus the churning started.

The churning! It created a poison at first. "It would destroy all! Where is it to be kept?" They were in a fix and then Lord Shiva swallowed it. He did not let it pass beyond his throat and so his neck became blue. Hence his name Nilakantha- the blue necked one. Thereafter poverty rose from the waters. Thus poverty, penury and all kinds of miseries, like hunger and thirst, obtained a goddess of their own named Jyeshtha, the Great or Eldest. Whereupon came Mahalakshmi, the goddess of wealth, to shower happiness and prosperity. Many other beings also came forth.

The story goes that at last they obtained the nectar. The nectar! It was kept in a jar by the gods and hidden in a secret place, guarded by

---

1. but not by books in the vernacular
2. gods
3. non-gods

the sun and the moon. The non-gods came to understand that the gods were going to deceive them. Thus deceiving the gods, as is their wont, the non-gods stole away the nectar-jar. Of course, the gods came to know of it and followed them. Running and running, the one after the other. Tiredness came upon the *asuras* as a friend of those who followed, helping them to retrieve the nectar which gives immortality. Thus the *asuras* made their first halt, and the jar of nectar was put down while they rested; that place is now known as Hara Charanam and Haraki Pairi, the feet of Hara. Hara is the Lord who dispels all afflictions and gives immortality. Hara Charanam - that place is Hardvar!

Hardvar! Thousands of people assemble there once in a year, and millions of people take a bath at the exact time of this historical event, once in every six and twelve years. From all over India people assemble there. This is known as the *kumbhamela*. The *kumbhamela*! It is a great national festival of India. The Haraki Pairi is a small lake remaining as a close associate to the river Ganga. Between the lake and the Ganga there is a platform, beautifully built, where people assemble to bathe and worship. There are many temples around it.

The history of the churning and the *kumbhamela* have a great significance. It has a spiritual interpretation. Meru, the mountain, is the spinal cord, and the serpent used as a rope is called the prana, the bio-energic force. The gods and non-gods are the *antahkarana chatushtaya* - ego, intelligence, mind and memory and the senses respectively. The fluid flowing through the ventricles is the milky ocean and the result is the nectar. The bitter poison is the ego, the faculty of identification; it destroys the whole world. Hara, the supreme Lord, retains it. The Haraki Pairi, the lake, is the *hrdayakasa*; that exact spot represents the *sushumna*. And taking a bath there means remaining in *samadhi*. The nectar is the knowledge of the eternal and non- eternal. *Kumbha* means a pot or a jar and symbolises the head, and the "*mela*" is the assembly of the senses, mind, memory, ego and intelligence. This represents the state of *pratyahara*; whereas the churning process is the *pranayama*. The sun and the moon are the *ida* and the *pingala*. Once in twelve years is equivalent to the time to attain *samadhi*; one needs twelve years constant practice of *yogangas* for this. Whereas the *yogi* is able to attain *yoganga-samadhi* after sitting at one stretch for twelve hours. To attain *pratyahara* needs six years practice. This is the spiritual interpretation of the *kumbhamela*. As a national festival it demonstrates the purpose of Bharatiya Rashtriyatha, Indian nationhood, as Self-realisation through self-restraint and through the practice of *yogangas*. Because of this reason all the saints, sages and savants will assemble there during this festival. It is the most authentic proof to justify the spiritual interpretation of the festival.

The running away with the nectar is the state of *vyutthana* in which one cannot proceed further. Only by attaining the culminent intelligence as a result of the *yoganga-samadhi*, with which the student of the *Yoga-sutras* is well acquainted, are all the afflictions destroyed and is immortality attained. This is represented by the resting of the jar at the feet of Hara.

Hardvar is thus enriched with a spiritual and traditional glory and intertwined in the national life of Bharata, India. Hardvar stands as the divine mother, or the Citishakti of the *Yoga-sutras*. Hardvar is the city of temples, whose population are worshippers of God who aspire to attain heaven, or to see God or to realise the Self. The Ganga! with her majestic and pompous flow, her dancing bubbles and rolling waves is where the devotees assemble in the evening and where they leave burning lamps, made in leaf-goblets filled with rose petals, on the river. These float like tiny boats and it appears as if the setting sun dwells in them and is flirting on the rolling waves of the majestic flow of the Ganga.

Saints were sitting for meditation on the river-bank, in the midst of the people singing hymns in praise of God and ringing bells in the temples. The whole of Hardvar appeared at the time of sunset completely merged in prayer and meditation. The sun, as usual, undertook its evening duty to sprinkle golden paint on the trees and the plants, on the mountains and the clouds, just before setting. The sun set and the darkness came just like the disappearance of the wise brings darkness to the people.

The twilight in Hardvar! It was like the twilight of the mundane and divine life. It shows the incapability of mundane life to exist. The saints and savants, literate and illiterate, poor and rich, *sannyasins* and householders, all alike, remained in prayer and meditation. All had withdrawn from the mundane activities of the day and become introspective. The moon, like the culminent intelligence of a *yogi*, slowly and steadily takes the place of the setting sun, dispelling the darkness of the night but creating confusion and doubts on certain occasions, like the *vyutthana* state of a *yogi* who is about to reach culmination. All the sweating and burning of the day in the scathing sun disappeared in the cool breeze and in the lovely and soothing beams of the moon. It gave a happiness to the mind and body, helping the devotees to have more concentration, like the thought of the greatness of tolerance and endurance while one is in a rage and emotional.

We both remained there in the midst of the divine people, in the atmosphere of peace and tranquillity until nine in the evening. Then, as *Svamiji* suggested, we left for the other side of the river. We spent the night there in meditation and sleep. We used to sleep only two hours and spent more time in meditation and discussion. *Svamiji* asked me about my study in *Vedanta* and *Yoga*. From my answer *Svamiji* said, "*Vedanta* is all right but the *Yoga* and *Sankhya darshana*[1] needs careful study and practice."

The next morning, from nine to eleven, after our morning duties and meditation, we started to discuss the *Yoga-sutras*, the aphorisms of *Yoga*. *Svamiji* could give me a clearer insight with his explanation of the subject and taught me how to practise accordingly; this is reflected later on in my commentary on the *Yoga-sutras* and *Vedanta*sara. During our discussion I mentioned to *Svamiji*, "Nowadays I think too often of my *guru*. I long for him, I have not had any contact with him for about one year. After his departure for Europe and America I commenced my wandering tour." *Svamiji* kept silent for a moment, closing his eyes, then he told me, "You couldn't understand what is happening. It is he who made me contact you. It is he who brought you to me. It is his desire that I should teach you the *Yoga- sutra*. He will be here within a fortnight. We should remain in Hardvar for a fortnight." So we both remained there, myself learning from him the difficult portions of the *Yoga-sutra*, morning and evening, eight hours a day. I was learning and practising according to

---

1. *darshana:* a school of philosophy

the *Yoga-sutras*. Learning in the morning and the same practising in the evening. It was the golden period of my life; I completely merged in study and practice. His method of teaching, his simplicity, discipline and freedom, his fearlessness and straightforwardness made a deep impact on me, which influenced me so powerfully that later on these became a part of my expression. When we are in association with others it may bring depreciation and non-acceptance from them. Therefore I asked him once, "What about the people, if we and other saints speak the truth, denouncing the superfluous expressions of the people, they will misunderstand." He replied, "The most unwanted things in the world are three: God, the truth and freedom though all people will speak in their name. So hold and speak what you think right in the light of the scriptures."

One day, at noon, after our lesson, we went to Kankhal where many large *ashrams* were built by various great saints and *acharyas*, standing as a storehouse of knowledge and saints. Kankhal, as that of Hardvar, has a great history which tradition has passed down to the modern generation. There was once a great Prajapati known as Daksha. Prajapati means the Lord of the people and he is one who protects the people; this is the correct meaning of the word. This great Prajapati Daksha had twenty-one daughters whom he had given in marriage to different gods. The youngest one, Sati, was given to Lord Shiva. A few years after this, Daksha performed a very great sacrifice for which he invited all his daughters and sons-in-law except Sati and Lord Shiva, because Shiva did not attire in royal garments but in elephant or tiger skin. He had serpents as his ornaments and a crescent moon on his matted tresses, had three eyes and spent his nights in the cemetery, besmearing his body with the ashes of the burnt remains. This is how he is understood and described in the mythology.

Sati, the youngest and dearest to her parents, had chosen Lord Shiva herself and had been given by her parents to Lord Shiva in wedding, even though Daksha did not like the choice, simply because Lord Shiva did not fit in well in the company of his other sons-in-law of regal splendour and royal dignity. But, though uninvited, Sati felt an uncontrollable longing to be present at the celebration of the great sacrifice of her father. Lord Shiva tried to persuade her not to go, yet she wanted to. So he gave her permission to be present and sent her to her parents accompanied by his entourage. Surprisingly enough, upon seeing her, Daksha did not even talk to her, not to speak of offering her a place to stay. She was completely neglected and insulted. Thinking of the humiliation from her parents, and the ignominious treatment accorded to her, compelled her to take a decision not to return to her husband. And she left her body by the power of *Yoga*. Upon hearing this news Lord Shiva, in extreme anger, ran to Daksha's palace, along with his entourage, and ordered them to destroy the entire sacrifice, while he separated the head of Daksha from his body with his sword. Thus he brought the sacrifice to an end in the presence of all the emperors, kings, *rishis*, saints, savants, *brahmanas*, and the gods and nymphs of heaven. Lord Shiva then took the body of his beloved and danced. Seeing the situation and realising the greatest blunder and sin that had been committed by Daksha, in spite of his wisdom, all the gods, *rishis* and savants assembled there, sung some hymns in his praise and requested Shiva to bring Daksha back to life and let him continue the sacrifice. Anger cannot last for a long time in a wise person and Lord Shiva came down from his anger. Pleased with the dignitaries present there, he fulfilled their request by keeping a goat's head on Daksha's neck and then brought him into life[1], and the sacrifice was performed. It is this Sati who entered into the womb of Mena, the queen of the Himalayan king Himavat, and was born as their daughter who was later on known as Parvati or Girija and then became the wife of Lord Shiva again. This is one of the important events of Kankhal, Kankhal being the capital city of Daksha.

Kankhal! Like Hardvar, it also has great significance and tradition of the *dharma* in the land. It has a holy past, enriched with inspiring events, with many dharmic events, many mundane and divine events, and elevating and emancipating events. It is full of temples and *ashrams* of *sannyasins* and *yogis*; there is also a hospital, besides many *Ayurvedic* dispensaries. The hospital is the first of its kind in the place and established and run by the Ramakrishna Math. It is known as the Ramakrishna Sevasadan, hospital. The monks of the mission are doing service along with the other doctors and workers. It is the first

---

1. Daksha's head had been burnt and the goats' head is symbolic of his stupidity.

of its kind because no *sannyasins* do this kind of services normally. But when the government fails, saints should take up the task. That is the tradition in India. The hospitals, schools and colleges are the duties of the government for which the people pay taxes and revenues. But unfortunately the government used all its power to extract money from the people and then that money is used to concentrate the power further. Thus the poor people had to suffer from want of education and medical treatment. The best education and allopathic treatment were given to the people in the large cities by the British empire according to their wit and whims. There used to be an imperialistic humour and sarcasm in their pattern of imparting of education and medical treatment. There are still other centres of medical treatment and education run by Christian missionaries with the motto "Conversion through service". Therefore, under the inspiring guidance and leadership of the great Hindu *sannyasin* Swami Vivekananda, the hospitals in Kankhal and Benares continue to function just to bless the ailing population of these parts of the country. There are many *ashrams* of *sannyasins* where *Yoga* and *Vedanta* are taught regularly and systematically.

We went to just one of these *ashrams*. It was run by Swami Maheshvarananda who is next to none in his erudition and satsanga oratory, in his teaching and interpretation. It was the time when the class was going on. *Svamiji* was at his best; the subject was the metempsychosis. He was explaining the aphorism of the great Badarayana's *Vedanta-sutras* "*tadantara pratipatau ramhati samparishvaktah prasnaniruparabhyam*"[1]. A *sutra* completely dealing with metempsychosis. The sutra clearly refers to the questions and answers between the great king Pravahana and the yet to be Upanishadic *rishi* Shvetaketu and his father Aruni[2]. The story goes that after completing his education, as was the tradition, Shvetaketu went to the king for *bhiksha*, alms. Then the king asked him, "Have you completed your education?" "Yes", he replied. Then the king put the question, "Do you know where the soul goes after death?" "I don't know", he replied. Whereupon the king asked, "Do you know what the

---

1. III, i, 1, *Vedanta-sutras*
2. also known as Gautama

51

pitriyana and *devayana* are?" "I don't know", he said. Thereupon he came back to his home and asked his father about it. He said, "My dear son, had it been known to me, I would have taught you; now let us both go to that great king and learn it." They both went to the king to receive this knowledge. By tradition knowledge was not imparted so soon as it is done today in these modern times. One had to undergo a strict discipline for at least twelve years. But the king told them, "As you are *Brahmins* and have been practising austerities so many years, three years will be long enough. So be here and then I will impart it to you." Both the son and father, Shvetaketu and Aruni, remained there, anxiously longing for the opportunity to receive that knowledge, like a farmer is anxiously waiting for rain for cultivation. The following dialogue between the king, Shvetaketu and Aruni bears the testimony to the science of metempsychosis. These questions and answers are hinted at, here in the "*prasna nirupana*", questions and analysis.

We heard the *Svamiji* teaching this *sutra* very interestingly. My desire to study the *Brahma-sutras* was awakened. The talk was so beautiful and every aspect of it was being interpreted. There were twenty-five *sannyasins*, and ten *vanaprasthas*, husbands and wives who had retired to the forest for learning and practising *yoga* after their family life. It was a long class and concluded just before the bell rang for dinner. We had our *bhiksha* in the ashram. We both met Swami Maheshvarananda Giri and had a light conversation with him. I had Pythagorean views of metempsychosis and was also referring to the philosophy of Socrates, Kant and Schopenhauer. *Svamiji* was very interested. Just before his siesta we left him, but he asked us to remain there for a few days and meet him again in the evening. In my continuous conversations with him for three or four days I understood that my knowledge of oriental and occidental philosophy, which I had learnt, was not only not enough but completely a mass of husk; it did not have any substance. He advised me to learn the *Brahma-sutras sharirakabhasya*, the celebrated commentary of the omniscient Shankara, the Bhagavat Pujyapada. Then we left for Hardvar again. The time had come for *Guru-purnima*. The thundering clouds, occasional rains and lighting were like the wise man's hammering, anger and abuses.

I was a little disturbed because my *Gurudev* was expected within four days. We did not know anything of his programme and I was very anxious to see him. It so happened that all my spiritual brothers and sisters had also come to Hardvar, so I asked them, "What made you to come?" They replied, "We have an urge to come to Hardvar, since the day before yesterday, thus we came." Nobody knew our *Guruji's* programme. Then we thought of spending our days together. I introduced them all to the *Svamiji* who was with me. *Svamiji* was very happy and said, "There is a *samadhi* in the *Yoga-sutras* known as *dharma-megha samadhi*, in which all the impressions which are left to be destroyed and abandoned are burnt, and all the activities of the ego are culminating in that state. That *samadhi* is called *dharma-megha samadhi* which means "the clouds of *dharma*", signifying the knowledge of the substratum, the absolute, standing as a cloud just about to rain. Similarly, all of you are being assembled here like clouds waiting for the showering of knowledge and that will come from your *Gurudev*, whom I compare here with the *dharma-megha samadhi*."

The next day, while we were sitting on the bank of the river Ganga during the intervals of rain, we were all thinking of our *Guruji's* presence, anxiously longing, like Europe is longing for the sun in winter. Suddenly and surprisingly, I received a fine knock at my back. I found our *Gurudev* standing there. Of course, our position was exactly such as described in the Shrimad Bhagavata Purana.

AJĀTA PAKSHĀ IVA MĀTARAM KHAGĀH
STANYAM YATHĀ VATSATARAH KSHUDHĀRTHĀH
PRIYAM PRIYĀYĀH VYUSITĀ VISANNĀ
MANDRAVINDĀKSHA! DIDRKSHATE TVĀM

"As the little birds, whose wings are yet to grow, are longing for their mother; as the hungry calves are longing for the milk of the mother; as the beloved is longing to meet her lover who is away from her since long, so our mind, O the lotus-eyed, our mind is longing for you!"

We all had been equally longing for him. "How did you all manage to be here together? What is this conspiracy all about?" he joked at us.

So we replied, "Some invisible power forced us to be here. We were just discussing *Guru-purnima*." He said smilingly, "*Guru-purnima* is a wrong composition of words. What have you decided?" he asked. So I replied, "We have decided to be decided by you." Then he said, "Let us go to Hrishikesh, there we shall have our *caturmasi*, the four months' stay at one place." And surprisingly he told us that we would take up the *Brahma-sutras* for discussion. I was so happy to hear this; this was what I wanted. When I was about to introduce the *Svamiji* who was with me, he said, "I know him; no more introduction is needed." But he commented, "You are fortunate to have his company. I wanted you to meet him. Now let us proceed to Hrishikesh."

We went to Hrishikesh on foot. On the way we halted at the *Kali-kamblivala-sattram*. A century ago there lived a great saint in Hrishikesh, named Svami Vishuddhananda Sarasvati. He became known as Kalikamblivala because he did not wear anything else except a black blanket, *kalikambli*. So the people knew him as the man wearing only a black blanket; hence the name Kalikamblivala. He was a great sannyasin, adored by all *sannyasins*. It is he who commanded a *satram* to be opened where free accommodation and food is to be given to *sannyasins* and others. We were very happy to be there, but our *Gurudev* never remained in houses nor in rooms but always in the open air - in the rain, in the sun and in winter. All the comfort and convenience was meant for us. On the second evening we reached Hrishikesh. In Hrishikesh, on the other side of the river Ganga, was a famous place known as the Svargashram and just up in the woods on the hills, *Guruji* ordered us to build a temporary hut. We made some small huts at his command, and a larger one for the *satsangas*. In two days we had completed the task of construction, just enough to protect from the rain. The long cherished day of fulfilment approached and we were now busy in arranging the ceremony and celebration for *Guru-purnima*.

The *Guru-purnima*! The most auspicious *purnima*! The *purnima* which has the privilege of dispelling the darkness of ignorance. All other *purnimas* may dispel the darkness but not the ignorance. This particular *purnima* occurs once a year. This *purnima* has the privilege of having the *guru* as its presiding deity. This is the important and pertinent aspect of it.

The *tithi, paksha* and *masa* are very important in the celebrations and ceremonies for the Hindus. A *tithi* is any day of the *paksha* and a *paksha* is any fifteen days of a month. Sometimes a *paksha* may also be fourteen or sixteen days; this depends upon the position of the stars. *Paksha* means a part and *tithi* means a day associated with any one of the twenty-seven significant stars. The Hindus generally follow the lunar system; their months and days are formed according to the position of the moon, *indu*, and therefore Bharata Varsha, India, was known in ancient days as Indurashtra; both *varsha* and *rashtra* mean country or nation. The word India is derived from this word *indu*. The weeks and days, such as Sunday and Monday, are of later origin. These days and weeks were not found, at least not by myself, in the Hindu scriptures and *Puranas*. Among the *tithis*, the first is called *prathama* or *pratipada*, and the *ashtami*, eighth day, and the *chaturdashi*, the fourteenth day, along with the *amavasi*, black moon day, are considered inauspicious and declared holidays for students and teachers. There is a verse concerning them:

AṢṬAMI CA GURŪM HANTI
ŚISYAN HANTI CATURDAŚĪ
AMĀVĀSYOBHAYAM HANTI
HANTI PĀTHĀN PRTIPADĀḤ

"The teaching during the astami day (the eighth day of the paksha) will destroy the guru, and the chaturdashi the disciple. Both the guru and disciple are destroyed by teaching on the amavasi (dark moon day). The lessons are destroyed on the prtipada (the first day of the tithi)"

It means that by teaching on the eighth day, when the moon comes exactly in the middle, which influences the intelligence, one will not be capable of imparting knowledge because of the influence of the moon. The fourteenth day is almost darkness and so the disciple's mind will be sporting; hence ego and the like will develop. Thus it is not good for the disciple to learn on that day. The day of the black moon is completely to be avoided because it comes very close to the earth and influences the mind of the teacher and the taught. The first day is the same. I do not know much about this science but this is how I understand it; it may be right, it may be wrong.

Thus the *purnima* is not to be abandoned. Not only does the moon shine in full brilliance but it influences the mind completely by helping the concentration. Thus blessed with this and many other auspicious qualities the *purnima* occupies a very important place in the life of the Hindus.

The *purnima* in the month of July is generally celebrated only among the intelligentsia, especially among the *darshanikas*, philosophers. It was my first occasion and opportunity to celebrate the day, worshipping the *guru* and receiving new instructions from the *guru*. This is the day that the *guru* becomes a very good task master. *Gurudev* made us to sit for meditation for at least four hours and many were frightened of the marathon-sitting. The previous day of the *purnima*, *Gurudev* spent his whole night in meditation and worship while the disciples were busy preparing the worship of their *guru*.

The seat! The seat on which the *guru* should sit! It is one meter high and covered with the *kashaya vastra*, a specially coloured cloth of which the colour is an imitation of the flames of fire. The necessary things for the *purnima* are: sandalwood paste, vermilion, *akshadam*[1], turmeric powder, loose flowers and flower garlands. After the worship, the disciples, according to their merit and rank, wash the feet of the *guru*, first with water, then with milk and curd and then again with water. After drying the feet, first the sandalwood paste is applied on the toes of the *guru* and then the *akshadam*, mixed with the vermilion and turmeric powders, and the flowers. This is followed by prostrating unto his feet. Thereafter fragrant incense and *dipam*, oil-lamp, are shown to him in a circling motion while singing *Vedantic* hymns. This is the ceremony and after this a *satsanga*, discourse, begins. The *guru* will explain the oneness of *Brahman* and Self. Thereafter dinner and then rest. In the evening at six o'clock the meditation starts and continues until 10 o'clock. These are the functions of the day. These are the ceremonies of the *Guru-purnima* and this is how it is celebrated. In the absence of the *guru* his picture is used and worshipped.

---

1. unbroken rice fresh from the husk

The *Guru-purnima* is also known as *Vyasa-purnima*, after the great Badarayana who systematically compiled the *Vedas* into four: the *Rg, Yajus, Sama* and *Atharva Veda*. The *Rgveda* consists predominantly of hymns, the *Yajus* of prose, the *Samaveda* of songs and music and the *Atharvaveda* is a mixture of all these three. These are the four *Vedas* named by Badarayana, Vyasa.

The next day after the *purnima*, though we had all abandoned our sleep the previous night, we were very smart and alert. According to the tradition we worshipped the *guru* and were very eager to listen to his talk. He enlightened us on the meaning of *"tattvamasi"*, quoting a verse from the *Vivekacudamani* of the omniscient Shankaracharya, Bhagavat Pujyapada[1].

JĀTI NĪTI KULA GOTRA DŪRAGAM
NĀMA RŪPA GUNA DOSA VARJITAM
DEŚA KĀLA VISAYĀTIVARTI YAD
BRAHMA TATTVAMASI BHĀVAYĀTMANI

"Which is devoid of species, creed, family, lineage, devoid of name and form, merits and demerits transcending space, time and sense-objects. That Brahman thou art; on this contemplate within."   *Vivekacudamani,* Verse 254

Gurudev explained in detail the entire topic dealing with *"tattvamasi"* as mentioned in the *Chandogya Upanishad* and analysed the meaning of the words *tat, tvam* and *asi*[2], using the method of *Vedanta,* such as the commencement and conclusion, repetition and originality, the result, eulogy and demonstration. *Asi* denotes the uncontaminated presence; *tvam* denotes the conditioned object as a being and *tat* denotes the unconditioned being. What makes them to be a being, conditioned or unconditioned? That is the "is", the

---

1. The latter is the name given to him by his *guru*, Govinda-pada, after initiating him into *sannyasa*. His disciples added the word *pujya*, to be adorned, before the word *pada*.

2. that, you and is (thou art that)

presence. The *tat* and *tvam* exist as presence because they are both present at all time, whether in a conditioned or in an unconditioned form. That presence is the existence; that is the consciousness; that is the bliss. The present, *asi*, denotes the absolute existence-consciousness-bliss. The *tat* and *tvam*, irrespective of their attributes and characteristics, are the absolute existence-consciousness-bliss; they are one and the same. We were asked to meditate upon that.

The next day *Gurudev* started to explain the method of meditation upon the *Udgitha*, called the *Udgithopasana*, as mentioned in the *Chandogya Shruti*. The method of pronunciation of *OM* in a long, longer and longest manner and of the meditation while following this process. The sound itself is to be reduced from gross to subtle, from subtle to subtler and then to be dissolved into the cause. In *Vedic* terminology it is called *udata-anudata-pluta* which means long, longer, longest. Concentrating on the subtle body the gross body should be negated, concentrating on the causal body the subtle body should be negated and concentrating on the *Atman*, the Self, the causal body should be negated, while reciting the *mantra OM* in long, longer and longest metres respectively. This concentration should succeed spontaneously one after another as also the repetition of the *Udgitha*. This brings *samadhi* in quick succession. It was very interesting and inspiring to practise in solitude, together with so many spiritual aspirants belonging to the same school and practising under the same preceptor. After spending a few days in the solemn atmosphere, we had the privilege to enjoy the sanctum sanctorum of life in the midst of the trees and bushes of the Himalayan valleys, graced by the snow-clad peaks of the majestic Himalayas, and the pompously flowing Ganga fertilising and sanctifying the river bank on both sides and producing the *Udgitha* itself, while the rocking racks of clouds were drizzling.

From there we came down to the Svargashram, where we had a very good feast arranged by the devotees; besides us more than one hundred *sannyasins* took part. It is the tradition that during the collective dinner, while the food is served, the *sannyasins* repeat the fifteenth chapter of the *Bhagavad Gita* to give the dignity and glory of a *yajna* to the taking of meals. A *yajna* is a sacrifice which is performed as an offering to God. The body is considered to be a *mandira*, temple, wherein the conditioned *Ishvara*, God, resides in the form of the self-luminous Self, illuminating the gross body or gross senses through the causal and subtle bodies. When one contemplates on the luminous Self while taking food, the food becomes purified and produces a good mind and body. How the presence of the Self illuminates the causal, subtle and gross bodies is explained in the fifteenth chapter. The recitation of this particular chapter is not only a reminder of the Self - the illuminator of the senses and bodies - but also purifies the atmosphere and transforms the food by offering it to God as a *yajna-shishtah*, the balance left after the performance of a *yajna* which is considered to give the effect of immortality.

After the food we had a nice time gossiping. Sitting together in small groups we were discussing, sometimes satirically, sometimes with wit and humour, the subject that we had been taught and also all we had heard, seen and experienced within these past days, casting various reflections on the different aspects of our experiences.

At that moment a poor family, a husband, wife and four children, came there for food. In India there are many poor people begging, as victims of the accumulation of wealth, which started during the Mogul period and which attained its climax during the British period, giving birth to many feudalists and capitalists. Formerly only the *brahmins* and *brahmacaris*, celibates, being the students of the *Vedas* and other material of spiritual subjects, as well as the *sannyasins* would go for *bhiksha*, requesting alms from householders as their righteous duty or *dharma*. As the feudalistic and capitalistic system developed under the protection of the then prevailing governments, there was no possibility of exploiting the resources for agricultural purposes. This gave birth to laziness and poverty. Then the poverty stricken people used to shelter under the umbrella of *bhiksha*, requesting alms as a righteous duty. Thus, poor people are now used to come to where *sannyasins* assemble and where brahmins perform *yajnas*, not because of any desire for spiritual emancipation but because, having faith in God, they know that the people who believe in God will give something to eat when they come and beg. Of course they have great faith in *sannyasins*.

When the family were taking food, one of the children suddenly became unconscious due to epilepsy. The boy was sixteen years old.

It was a terrific scene and everybody was worried. Someone went to call doctors, but the doctors could not cure; they gave certain suggestions and some medicines, just to receive some money for their visit. When *Gurudev* had awakened from his meditation he was walking among some of the *sannyasins* and householders and was told of this event by one *sannyasin*. Immediately he rushed to that family and saw the boy. He took the boy, made him to stand and asked him to practise certain *pranayamas*. He gave the boy a little juice of a herb and told him, "This will never come to you again!" We never knew before that *pranayama* could cure epilepsy. The herbal medicine given to the boy was meant to help recover his physical strength lost by the attack so to enable him to practise the *pranayama* according to the instructions. It was really an inspiring and encouraging experience for us regarding the efficacy of *pranayama*. Since then we were very much interested to learn various kinds of *pranayamas* and their different methods.

From Svargashram and after the rainy season we left for Vasishtha Guha, the cave of Vasishtha, en route to Uttarakashi which literally means "northern kashi", whereas the householders left for their homes. It was a thirteen miles walk. A walk with the *Guru*. A walk through the valleys of the Himalayas. A zigzag journey with ups and downs over tiny hills which stood like small knuckles of the Himalayan fingers. We were all walking with slow and steady steps in deep contemplation on what *Gurudev* would say. He walked like a flying saucer, was always a tiring distance ahead. As his thoughts, so his steps, always at an unreachable height and distance away from our level and ability. But as if inspired by God, listening to our prayers, he used to wait for us. Thus we reached Vasishtha Guha by noon.

In the meanwhile, on our way, we had some chit-chatting. He told us, "Have you marked the running horse? When a horse is running, it looks straight. When it wants to look around it stops a while and then again runs fast. It is of the nature of *rajoguna*. The horseman controls it with his knowledge of riding. Knowing the various techniques of how to control a horse, the horseman regulates the motion of the horse and stops it when he wants. Similarly, the running mind is to be controlled by proper discrimination with the intelligence. Otherwise the mind will stop all progress with its doubts and confusions, looking around for an answer to its problems in confusion and despair. The intelligence alone can guide the senses and the mind. Therefore one should control the mind with proper discrimination. If one did not learn and develop this method of discrimination and discernment, one will always be lost in the wide and wild world." On another occasion he said, "He who thinks that he knows everything knows nothing." Then I asked him, "Why should one think like that?" "Because," he replied, "he fears that he will lose his individual interest by following others' advice and therefore the best and most powerful fort he could construct around himself is his inferiority complex which always assumes the form of superiority and aggressiveness. I know that the one simple sentence which consoles him is "I understand everything"; this is a panacea to protect his ignorance." At some other time he told us, "The people in general who want to pose themselves as wise and pure, practise ritualistic cleanliness, purity and austerity while their mind is like a forest infested with wild animals and poisonous reptiles. You mark the ritualists, in the end, they can never become humane. Kindness and compassion are the products of discrimination and discernment, otherwise, in their absence, love, kindness and compassion will become a weakness, never a virtue. To see God, to talk to him, to be with him, just to have some gossip, to attend upon him as servants, and the like, are dangerous sentiments and attitudes and very difficult to cure. It is a clever escape from one's responsibility and from one's commitments and crimes. God does not need any servant to attend upon him, nor has he any needs at all. He commands none but is present in everyone and everywhere. To know him one should learn the method of how to know him, like one learns how to use the herbs in the Himalayan mountains. All along our way we have seen so many herbs and plants but we know only very few of them. There are herbs which can cure all kinds of illnesses, but we don't know them. Such herbs are present everywhere. Similarly, in one's own body there are many techniques to produce many illnesses, which people practise without any teacher. But at the same time, to cure all diseases, there are many medicines side by side in the body of man. To find out the remedy, one needs discrimination, and study of his own body. You see no *yogi* suffer from illness. If he does, he is able to cure himself. Similarly, God is present everywhere; it is due to our ignorance that we could not realise it; one cannot see God living in God. It is just like when one is in the ocean and then tries to see the ocean; or when we are walking on earth through space and we then try to see the space by looking above us as if we are not in space already ourselves. One should understand God, what it is, and realise it."

After this there was a silence for a while and I broke it by putting a question to the beloved *Gurudev*. "Why then do some of the *yogis* or *sannyasins*, some of the *gurus*, suffer from illnesses?" After a small pause he asked us to sit down on the ground. The place where we sat was very beautiful, of course, as beautiful as any other place in the Himalayan valleys. As we had walked a long distance, for a few miles, sitting gave us an opportunity to view the valley and its scenery. There was sunshine. There was no river nearby but there were small villages with a few inhabitants. The grazing cows, the milking cowherds, the crying, running and jumping calves provided an atmosphere in which we became lightning-like visitors. We all observed, in that silent solitude, that *Gurudev's* presence gave a magnificent magnitude of spiritual and divine sublimity.

His long beard, uncared-for loose hair, tall and slim body, with the *kamandalu* and deerskin that he always carries along with him, give us the impression of an ancient saint, of an ancient rishi of wisdom. He has a musical tone, is very accurate in his accents and every sentence that he utters is grammatically accurate and punctual. When one happens to hear him, one will take it for granted that he is a great grammarian. Slow but spontaneous his expression reflects conviction and confidence in what he says. He won't utter a word which has not the support from the scriptures and experience of *sannyasins* like Shankara and others. That makes him very clear and understandable but at the same time his bold statements put us in confusion regarding some of the well-known modern saints. Therefore I have put the question above.

Steadily and slowly he replied, "A *yogi* never suffers. He has no illness. Of course, there are certain *sannyasins* and *yogis* who live in the cities, enjoying comforts and forgetting their daily duties. They have to suffer because they eat and drink like householders. They receive offerings in the form of money, land and so on from the rich. These all contain sins. The food to be taken is what one receives as *bhiksha*. If the *yogi* or *sannyasin* takes only that food they will never fall ill. If one collects food, even for the evening, it is a sin. They are bound to fall ill. It is against the principles of *Yoga*. The body is made of *prarabdha*. This *prarabdha* is always ready to grab the health. It can be blocked when the mind never makes any contact with the body. And by the practice of concentration the *prarabdha* can be destroyed. As this is not done, they have to suffer. Realisation of the Self destroys the *prarabdha* completely. After one has attained *samadhi* and continues to remain in it, maintaining all the rules practised to attain Self-realisation, no illness will come to him. I mean, the practice of *yogangas* is essential until one attains *samadhi*. After attaining *samadhi*, in the state of *vyutthana* (the state when one comes out of *samadhi*) one should follow the practice of *yogangas*. Then alone can one be free from all afflictions. Otherwise, it is impossible to escape from illnesses and the defects of old age. Not practising the *yogangas* is the cause of illness for such *yogis* and *sannyasins*. Attachment is another cause for illness. This brings laziness. *Tamoguna* will catch him. The attachment in any form is comforting to the senses. The senses feel comforted only in inaction. Inaction is the property of *tamoguna* when predominant. Postponement of practice, not taking care of one's food habits and so on are its results. Though they suffer from various illnesses it does not mean that they are not *yogis*. It only shows that they do not practice the *yogangas* at present and do not follow strictly the sanctions of the Yoga-sutras and *Vedanta* in their life."

After drinking some water from our *kamandalus* we left for Uttarakashi. On the way we halted in a small village which had a population of about fifty or sixty people. We made our shelter under a tree for the night. After some time when they saw us sitting there, the villagers came to us and requested us to sleep in their house. Their houses were very small and hardly three or four persons could be accommodated but they had some tents which they provided for us. As we did not take any cooked food in the evening they provided us with milk and bananas. After our evening meditation all the villagers collected around us and asked us to visit their homes. There is a belief among Hindus that if saints visit their homes, their poverty and illness will be removed. During our visit in one of the houses we found a woman suffering from delivery pains. We were told that one week had passed since she began to suffer. They had approached doctors of some distant villages but as they could not make the payments of the doctor's fee and transport expenses, no medical aid was given. Her husband approached us asking us to give relief to his wife and to help her have a safe delivery. It was in the night; the night in the Himalayan valley means a terrible dense darkness, nothing can be seen, not even at the closest distance. We then saw our *guruji* leaving the place and after moving about on the outskirts of their hutment. He then returned with some medicines. He asked her to smell the herbs and then gave a little juice of it for her to drink. Within fifteen minutes she had a happy delivery. The child was quite healthy. All the villagers were very happy. After some time and after visiting their houses, we returned to our camp.

The next morning, after our daily routine, when we opened our door, we found the entire village standing before us, all had some complaint to tell us. Our *Gurudev* smilingly told us, "We can't leave this place before twelve noon. It is a sin if we leave the village without bringing happiness to them." So *Gurudev* was busy sprinkling water while chanting *mantras*, to some persons he gave medicines and to some others his blessings. Thus, by eleven o'clock we did not find any more persons who made a complaint. Everyone was very happy. One among them put a question, "Would you please tell us some stories about God?" Another wanted a *mantra* for their daily prayer. That was a wonderful request. *Gurudev* asked us to give them a *mantra* and he started to tell some stories about God.

The story started. God has no form and yet, if you think of him in any form or person, he appears in that form. Once there was a big fight in heaven. The demons had attacked the heaven and the gods counterattacked. The fight was a very big one. The gods prayed to the Supreme God to bestow the victory on them. The result was that the gods won the battle; the demons were defeated and ran away from the battlefield. Sometime after the war, when they were in peace with the demons, the gods forgot all about the Supreme God. They were possessed by their ego; they all thought that the victory was due to their own skill and might. Thinking thus they became so egoistic that they forgot their meditation and prayer.

One day God assumed the form of a *Yaksha*, a being different from gods and men, having supreme powers, and appeared before the king of the gods, Indra. He did not pay any respect to Indra, the king of all the gods in heaven. Seeing him standing at a distance, paying no respect, Indra was surprised and desired to know who he was. Because of his ego and royal position, he did not go himself, nor could he understand who he was. So he asked the god of fire, Agni, to go to him and find out who he was. Upon approaching him the *Yaksha* asked, "Who are you and what is your power?" Agni replied, "I am the god of fire; I can burn any object in the world to ashes." On hearing this the *Yaksha* took a dry blade of grass and asked the god of fire to burn it; but he could not. Having failed and being disappointed and dejected he returned to Indra and told him of his plight and said, "I don't know who he is."

Indra was a little frightened. He thought that someone else had come to capture his throne. Giving no expression to his fear, he asked Vayu, the god of the wind to go to the *Yaksha* and ask him who he was. When Vayu approached him the *Yaksha* asked, "Who are you and what is your power?" "I can move any object in the world as fast as I want and I can uproot trees and break mountain- peaks", Vayu replied. The *Yaksha* took the same dry blade of grass, put it before him and asked him to move it. Vayu approached the blade of grass as fast as he could but failed to move that dry grass; that simple blade of dry grass the mighty Vayu could not move. Having failed, disappointed and demoralised, Vayu returned to Indra and said, "I don't know who he is; I am powerless in his presence."

Then they requested Indra himself to go and find out who this was. Indra got down off his throne, full of fear and doubt, and tried to go to the *Yaksha* but just at that moment the *Yaksha* disappeared. Seeing his sudden disappearance and realising that Agni and Vayu had been powerless in its presence, the ego of Indra was almost crushed. He was in a prayerful mood and prayed to the Supreme God to know the identity of the *Yaksha*.

Suddenly there appeared before him a very beautiful young girl, sixteen years of age, adorned with golden ornaments, who told Indra that the *Yaksha* was the Supreme God, *Brahman*, himself. Then she explained, "You won victory over the demons with his grace; without his grace all of you are as powerless as dry grass. In his presence even a dry blade of grass is much more powerful then anyone of you. Therefore, give up your ego and surrender to God. He alone is all-powerful and because of him every being has got life. He alone is the ruler of the universe. All of you are nothing but fools in his hand. Know this and be free from the chains of ego."

We left the village and continued our journey. Like the hide-and-seek game of children, the sun occasionally peeped through the black cloud. Sometimes it was hiding behind the cloud which sprinkled water on us as a warning that a torrential downpour was ahead of us. Folding and unfolding the umbrellas assumed the form of a new exercise and sport. At times the sun shone brilliantly and then suddenly disappeared. As soon as it disappeared, the rain fell. But we continued in solemn silence, through the trodden path of the cattle and cowherds, sheep and shepherds. We walked for an hour and then stopped for a cup of tea, just to cool our bodies.

Gurudev - 6'2" in height, long hair covering half of his back and his long silver beard hanging down to his navel, his broad forehead, long pointed nose, long ears, his calm and brilliant eyes, dwelling in quietude and compassion, his oval shaped face, his long arms stretching four fingers above his knees, his fair complexion, shining among his disciples as Brihaspati among the gods - the *guru* of the gods in heaven - sat down along with us and started to talk just to give us an opportunity to listen to his melodious voice. An attractive and influential sweet melody, that is his voice, none can become tired of hearing it, at least none among us. We never came across a similar voice, even from the greatest of musicians. I doubt how far the *Vina*, the highest instrument of Indian classical music, is capable of producing a sound so accomplished in its sweetness and kindness. He said, "Sorrows and happiness are commingled like darkness and sunshine in the rainy season. The *karmashaya*, the receptacle of acts, showers sorrows and happiness like rain. Sometimes it falls in torrents, sometimes it sprinkles. Sorrows come spontaneously, like happiness, not considering the occasion and place - similar to the clouds and the sun. We experience externally but relatively within, because all experiences are within. The external objects with which we have come into contact by the mind through the senses, are also dwelling within. Knowing that they are transitory, that they are coming and going, endure them, dwelling in the true Self." Pointing at the *Svamiji* who is with us, who had accompanied me all along, he said, "Look at him, he is the only one who doesn't shiver in the cool breeze and who doesn't shelter under an umbrella and whose face reflects a satisfaction. He is a living example of how *titiksha*, endurance, can bring happiness within."

I asked, "How is it possible to walk and concentrate on the Self within?" He replied, "It is most easy to do. What is the most difficult is that what you practise very easily; for instance while you walk or while you take tea, you talk about the mountains of Switzerland and compare the rain with that of Europe; now you think of Switzerland, of Europe, of the mountains. You concentrate on the mountains and rain of Europe while you are walking or drinking tea at the foot of the Himalayas in India. I was surprised how you could carry Europe along with its mountains and rain and yet you could walk and drink a cup of tea! You could do it because of your constant practice since childhood. Similarly, by the constant practice of *yogangas* or the *satsampattis* of *dama, shama, uparati, titiksha, shraddha* and *samadhana*, or the *shravana, manana* and *nididhyasana* you can do the same. While you walk, while you talk, while you eat, while you act you can function in the Self."

We have commenced our journey to Uttarakashi after a fifteen minutes' halt. By six in the evening we had reached Uttarakashi. The manager of the *Kali-kamblivala-sattram* kindly arranged our stay in a comfortable place, just above the river Ganga. After our supper and a cup of milk we sat for meditation. It was quite pleasant to practise a few *hathayoga* postures and *pranayamas* for half an hour before the supper. It was very helpful to remove all the fatigue after our long, five hours' walk through the short-cut routes.

Uttarakashi - it is called so because, as in Kashi, Benares, so here in this northern corner of the Himalayas, *sannyasins* of the highest order dwell here, studying and teaching and discussing the *prashtanatraya* in the light of the commentary of the omniscient Shankara. Uttarakashi is a small village with a small population and a large territory. People here dwell in the valley with their cattle-wealth, cultivating paddy and vegetables. They are a very happy people. They are not civilised or cultured in the sense that the people, who are drawn into industrial civilisation and culture, know of it. They do not have problems. They do not know much about the definitions of God, but they have an implicit faith in God. They have traditional social ethics and social ties. They know nothing about what is going on in the world nor are they interested to know. For transport, the bus reached here after the second world war and by 1957 there were one or two buses coming from Hrishikesh. After the Chinese invasion it obtained political and military importance. Hence, it started to grow very fast. I think it might have developed as a district-town by this time. There was a road being built towards Gangotri. I do not know whether it is completed or not. That small village might now have been civilised; the people might have learned the art of speaking lies and stealing and cheating as an essential part of the civilisation. The quietude and purity of Uttarakashi, if it has developed into a town, might have disappeared and it might have become a tourist centre like Hrishikesh, Hardvar and Benares.

It was very delightful to see small oil-lamps burning in the huts of the valleys, as if some of the twinkling stars have come down, leaving the blue sky, just to have an experience of earthly life. Perhaps the stars have become tired of a place where nothing grows, like on the top of a bald head. But for the burning oil-lamps and the silent whispering of the ever-flowing majestic holy river Ganga, the atmosphere remained quiet and calm like the mind of a *yogi* who is in the sixth state of *samadhi*, as mentioned in the *Yoga-sutras*.

At twelve in the night we saw our *Gurudev* sitting on a rock in the middle of the Ganga. The rock was two feet above the water. The moon shone slightly in between the clouds as if just to illuminate him to us in the dense darkness of the silent night. His grey hair and silver beard shone like reflectors in the moonbeams, but they were very obedient as they did not go beyond their border premises. At a few yards' distance there was a similar stone on which my companion and friend the Svamiji was sitting. From my room I was looking at them through my window, for a long time; I too attained concentration; I was merged into him. The *guru* - it is very pleasant to look at him, especially when he sits in meditation. After an hour I went to sleep.

The next morning when we all woke up we saw our *Gurudev* still sitting there as if somebody had placed another stone on that rock, an immovable object. Man could become more immovable than the rock, I thought. We bathed in the river Ganga, had our practice of asanas and our morning meditation. We had prepared a royal breakfast of a salty preparation of semolina, called *upma*, along with a cup of tea. *Gurudev* does not take all these, his greatest food is meditation, as if he knows nothing else to eat and drink. The *Svamiji* who was sitting by his side came out to take part in our breakfast. After breakfast we had a little talk about various subjects. Within our fifteen minutes' talk we touched on almost all subjects under the sun; we left the sun and the Himalayas untouched because the one is too hot and the other too cold.

"What next?" was our discussion. *Guruji* was still established in *samadhi*. Like honey bees we went around him dipping our *upma*-bellies in the water: a fresh exercise immediately after breakfast, in the cool morning. This morning was a little better than the previous one. It shone; it smiled and sometimes it laughed with the aid of the occasionally brilliant sun. Though the rain and the black clouds had disappeared in the other part of the country they persisted in the Himalayas, as if they were fond of Himalayan meditation. But they were very kind because the sky began to clear. As two hours passed we found that the atmosphere became a little warm. We sat around our *Gurudev* for some time, touched his feet with our heads and left. After returning to our ashram we decided to have a walk, individually, and return by eleven o'clock to prepare our dinner. I found a beautiful muddy road under construction. I just followed that road. The milestone showed sixty five miles to Gangotri. I followed the road for three and a half miles and then I saw a small ashram. I went there and saw a friend in the ashram, Gokula Chaitanya. Naturally I was very happy. He had been practising silence for twelve years and had now broken his silence some three months ago. That was the first time we both were talking to each other. Formerly he used to carry a slate and pencil to write a reply. He was practising *vastra-dhauti*, swallowing a strip of long cloth. I found some interest in that practice, so he taught me how to swallow it. That was very interesting. It was as difficult to swallow as an insult especially when it is openly met with. I learned it within five minutes. He was very happy that I could do it so quickly. He told me that it took him one week's practice to be able to swallow one yard of cloth. After some time I returned to the *ashram* where I reached by eleven o'clock. I found *Gurudev* still in meditation as if he was cemented to the rock. So we just started to cook the food, expecting that *Gurudev* would come to take food at twelve o'clock. We prepared kedgeree, a mixture of dal with two or three kinds of vegetable and rice and a little salt and tumeric powder; it made a sumptuous dinner. Food was ready exactly at twelve o'clock. We had our usual prayer before the meal and ate it satisfactorily while *Gurudev* was still in *samadhi*.

There was a whistling wind and the rain fell as if the clouds had lost their patience and started to shower its *karmashaya* on the earth. We thought that *Gurudev* might have come out of his *samadhi*; even after one hour heavy rain he was not in the mood to move at all. Then the *Svamiji* who was with us recited the famous Kalidasa's *Kumarasambhava*:

ĀTMESVARĀNĀM NA HI JĀTU VIGHNA
SAMĀDHIBHEDĀ PRABHAVO BHAVANTI

"There is nothing which is capable of breaking the state of samadhi of the yogi who is master of his mind and senses."

The rain came and left but *Gurudev* remained as before. The rest of the day there was good sunshine and we had no rain afterwards for a few days. I went to see Svami Vishnudevananda, the most honoured and respected by all for his learning and attainments in spiritual life. The moment he saw me, he took the *Brahma-sutras*, which were known to him by heart, and asked me to read the fourth commentary by the omniscient Shankara. He started to explain to me the intrinsic meaning of the first long sentence. It was much longer than the footpath from Hrishikesh to Uttarakashi but the sentences were very beautiful, like diamond necklaces, well presented in a manner sweet and delightful, yet deep, and indigestible to an average intellectual. He explained it to me in a most simple and beautiful style which I can never forget; I never knew that the highest *Vedantic* treatise could be explained in such a simple manner. He was a little old, lying down on his bed, sideways, his head raised with cushions, and his eyes closed. I could find in him the wisdom of the non-dualistic reality. He was a great saint, an authority of the time. When he stopped, we touched his feet and received his blessings. With his kind permission we said goodbye to him in a traditional way. Then we went to Svami Chetanananda Giri. Both Svami Chetanananda and Vishnudevananda had renounced their position as Mahamandaleshvara of Kailas Ashram in Hrishikesh. It appeared to me that Svami Chetanananda was much older. He gave a talk on "How to realise the Self" and it was inspiring and brilliant. One can seldom forget the impact of a talk by the great spiritual luminaries. When the talk was over he asked me all about my *Gurudev* and I touched his feet and received his blessings. When I said goodbye, he told us, "Generally we do not have rain in this time in Uttarakashi. Only this year it so happened. There will be no rain from now onwards."

We returned to our *ashram* after visiting one more *Svamiji*. *Gurudev* was still in *samadhi*. As per his order we took our supper and commenced our meditation. The next morning as usual we did our morning duties and had breakfast. Now the question arose, where to go next? When we were discussing this, *Gurudev* appeared before us and said, "Now all of you can return." So we decided to leave for Hrishikesh. *Gurudev* remained in Uttarakashi for some time. The *Svamiji* who was accompanying me all these months also remained there. The rest of us returned, some by a car of people who had come to visit Uttarakashi. By four p.m. we were in Hrishikesh.

A Solitary traveller

Alone in the multitude

Hardvar! The great Hara! Hardvar, meditating there one can realise the Hara. Hara means the destroyer of all afflictions and modifications; that is the Self. Hardvar! The place has its own sanctity and serenity. It has its own solitude and quietude; even today this is visible. In the midst of thousands of people, in the midst of many economical bargains, one can realise the most powerful solitude and quietude which is the very soul of Hardvar; it is still there in its magnanimous magnitude.

As in Hrishikesh so in Hardvar, the sectarian sentimentalism plays a very great role in confusing the inscriptions of the names of these places on stones and signboards: they write Haradvar and Haridvar instead of Hardvar. They do not write Hrishikesh but Rsikesh or Rishikesh instead, without knowing its meaning and history, which creates confusion among the species of tourists and human travellers, and among devotees. One can sometimes find them discussing and quarrelling about the names, about what is right and wrong. The credit for this goes mainly to the officials and officers of the public work department of Uttar Pradesh. Hrishikesh - the Lord of the senses! Rishikesh is a nonsense word which has not much meaning. Similarly with Hardvar.

We spent a day and night in Hardvar. At night I sat in meditation on the bank of the river Ganga. It was a very difficult experience. While trying to practise *pratyahara*, my mind was full of impressions of what I had heard and seen before. All the events of the association with my *Gurudev* and his other disciples, and of the *Svamiji* who accompanied me throughout, appeared one after the other, like twinkling stars appear in the blue sky one by one just after sunset. It took an hour and a half or even more to be successful in my pratyahara. I had to work very hard. The practice of *Samya-kumbhaka Pranayama* and *Yonimudra* helped me in my practice of *pratyahara*. Though I spent more than three hours, I was not successful in the concentration. On that night I had to be content with *pratyahara*. There were nice feelings in that state: quiet and calm, and all the impressions of the world remained within, without any contradictory functions. I thought it was a little like a hen collecting all her chickens under her wings, enjoying a deep sleep; the chickens, too, would be silent. This is how I felt at that moment. A complete disposition of activities and thoughts, just like Patanjali described it. The mind was fit for concentration in this state.

The dawn! The dawn appeared slowly and steadily with a smiling face like a sleeping baby waking up. It seemed to be similar to a *vyutthana samskara* appearing when one is free from concentration. Thus slowly and steadily the dawn was assuming various modifications and finally the gross form, what we call morning. The shining of the sun with its tawny rays falling upon everything, whatever was visible. Just like the *citta* of the *yogi* in *prasamkhyana samadhi* where the brilliance of the self-luminous Self floods the *citta*, illuminating all the objects fallen into it which remain subtle and unknown even in the *samadhi* known as *asmita*. I thought within myself that the process of the dawn becoming morning had taken place within me!

After my morning meditation which was better than the previous night, I met my spiritual brothers and sisters and had my breakfast with them. Then we discussed our programmes. I decided to remain in Hardvar for some more days and the others returned.

The moment! The moment which was the turning point in my ascetic life. Until that moment in my *sannyasa* life I had a long *dhoti* of five and a half yards, a *kaupina*, a *kamandalu*, one thick cloth, a long jute sleeping-sack and a staff as my possessions. The major portion of my time, that is sixteen hours per day and night, I spent in study and meditation. I did not entertain any visitors nor devotees; I preferred to study and meditate. I would spend two hours doing my morning duties. Very often I tried to be content with four hours sleep but generally I slept for six hours. Whenever I practised *Hathayoga* and some of the *shat-kriyas*, four hours sleep would be quite enough. During travelling I found it difficult to practise *Hathayoga*; then I needed six hours sleep. I used to take only fruit and milk in the morning and evening. At noon I would take rice. Somehow or the other, right or wrong, I gave more importance to cooking rice. I had the idea that rice was very good for the brain and that it gave a sharp intellect whereas wheat provided a strong body and a beautiful complexion.

During my three days' stay in Hardvar I heard many *sannyasins* and householders speak about a *sanyasin*. They spoke very highly of him. They held him in very high esteem. They adored him, they talked to me about him with great devotion and love, with admiration and adoration. They mentioned his name with worshipful respect. That prompted me to go and see him. He was staying at Saptasarovara. On the fourth day, after my morning duties, I proceeded towards him. I walked slowly. It took two and a half hours for me to reach his camp. When I reached him he was having his noon bath. He took a bath three times a day: at dawn, noon and in the evening. Just after his bath, before sitting for his worship, he called me and asked me about my *Gurudev* and myself. Then he told me to go and take my meal and then come back to him again. He asked one of his *brahmacharis* to provide me with food and to bring me back to him. He was a *yogi* of great insight.

That noon was a great surprise for me and revealing. During our talk he questioned me about everything that I had been practising, in detail, and the books which I had learnt. I was surprised that he asked me about the philosophy of Socrates, Plato, Pythagoras, Kant, Schopenhauer, Spinoza and Descartes, and above all he asked me about the modern philosophers' view on the soul, mind, ego, intelligence and *citta*. Then he remained silent for a few minutes. After this he wanted me to give a comparative presentation of eastern and western philosophies, in brief, and the quintessence of both. He asked me "Could you find a vast difference between the two schools of thought: Eastern and Western?" I said that there were many differences. He asked why there were these differences. I replied, "In the Western school they do not have the method of introspective inquiry to be able to know the internal functions of the human being. Theirs is an intellectual pursuit and they do not try to practise introspection or remain introspective. Hence a process is absent. But the more ancient the philosopher is the more subtle the intellectual perception is. I think that if they had continued the same method of intellectual pursuit, they might have discovered a certain definite process, such as a means conducive to reveal the truth within. Whereas the oriental philosophers have a process to experiment with the means conducive to the revelation of the internal truth such a *yama, niyama*, in the *Yoga*; *shama, dama* in the *Vedānta*; *asanas, mudras* and *shat-kriyas* in the *raja-yoga* and concentration on *chakras* in *kundalini-*

yoga." He sat quiet for a while and asked me, "Do you know what is meant by *adithi-bodhacharana-pracharah*, learning, understanding and reflecting upon what one has learned, practising of what is learned and propagating what is practised and understood according to learning?" I answered, "Yes, but I did not think of it so far. I am trying my utmost to practise that which I have learnt and understood for myself from the scriptures. I did not think of propagating at all." He said, "Do you know that you are protected by society, not by the law of the government but by the traditional moral code of the people in society. They give you food, clothes and shelter. What do you give them in return? If you don't think of the people and their welfare, while you expect them to think of your welfare and well-being then don't you realise that it is one-sided? Each one should be benefited by the other. That is the law of creation. Therefore it is necessary to propagate what you have learned." "Yes", I replied. My meeting with the great saint was over that day. He asked one of his disciples to accommodate me in her house. She was a very rich lady belonging to the family of the famous industrialist Ramakrishna Dalmia. That evening, before I fell asleep, I was thinking of the saint. When I left my *Gurudev* he had told me that I would meet a great *sannyasin* in Hardvar and be with him for some time.

Karapatriji! Karapatriji - that is how he was known. He was a medium sized person with a fair complexion, wearing only a *kaupina* and a *dhoti*. He had a *danda*[1]. He was sitting cross-legged, slowly swinging to and fro, with a small *rudraksha mala* around his neck. His forehead was besmeared with sandal-paste, a vermilion circle in the middle, with a shaven head. With his sparkling eyes and charming face he was ever unforgettable to a person who happened to see him once in his lifetime. He had a little stammer when speaking, but it was not easy to detect this. He was an eloquent orator of the highest calibre and could keep thousands of people spell-bound for hours. He was unparalleled in his learning and oratory in modern history. He was a very good debater and interpreter of the scriptures. He was a living authority on spiritual matters and on *Sanatana Dharma*, or the *dharma* of the *Vedas*, which is popularly known as Hindu *dharma*. He was a

1. stick

living embodiment of *Yoga* and *Vedanta*. He was a great exponent on *bhakti* and the *Puranas*. His favourite *Itihasa* was the *Ramayana* and his favourite *Purana* was the *Bhagavatam*. The former being the story of Rama, the latter being the story of Krishna. He was one of the arresting personalities of this century. None could defeat him in argument but he defeated all his opponents in debate. He could convince anyone to side with his point of view. As a politician he was a failure but as a *sannyasin* and *yogi* he was successful. His real name given by his *guru* was Hariharananda Sarasvati, but people called him Karapatriji because he took alms from the people's homes and ate from his palm. That is why he was called Karapatriji.

He was a fascinating personality. From the moment I met him I became very close to him. He gave me directions for my spiritual ambitions and cleared many of my doubts in relation to the scriptures. He explained to me many subtle aspects of Shankara's commentary on the *Brahma-sutra*. He guided me to the altar of worship. Before then I had never worshipped images of the gods. He rekindled the *bhakti*[1] and *advaita*[2] in the spiritual atmosphere of modern India. He ever remained a symbol of the orthodox spiritual life. He was the creator of the present Shankaracharyas in Northern India.

After leaving him I went to another spiritual luminary, Svami Krishnabodha Ashram, who was the Shankaracharya of Jyorthira Math at the time. It was the first time that I met him. He is obviously an elderly saint, with a clean mouth, no teeth left; yet he has a radiant smile. He is a personality of the highest calibre. In him one can find many of the characteristics of a *sthita prajna*, a *yogi* who is established in *Brahman*, as explained in the *Bhagavad Gita*. He is adorned with the qualities of *sadhana-chatushtaya*. Amongst scholars he is known as a mobile library; there is no scripture in the world which he does not know. He is a renowned and very respected personality in the spiritual India of today. After meeting him I had the privilege to be with him for a long time. During my travelling I used to meet him often. A pilgrimage to him was a great pleasure. On the occasions that we were alone he explained to me many of the apparent obscure *mantras* which

---

1. devotion
2. non-dualism

one can find in the *Bhagavad Gita* by exposing the hidden essentiality.

I had once been able to travel with him to Jaipur in Rajastan. He had been invited to preside over the annual gathering of the *Brahmashabha* there. In spite of the fact that he remained without food, he did not even eat a small fruit, he participated actively in the conference. His face, too, did not show a trace of weakness or tiredness. He remained himself; quiet and calm with a sparkling mind. Any person who would look at him would come under the influence of his radiant face. Most of the time he was in a state of *samadhi* which is the "wakeful state" for *sannyasins*. I owe part of my spiritual inheritance to him. He told me once that it is not so important to read the scriptures but that it is important to learn to understand what is meant by them. The notion of the truth only dawns when one understands the truth. To attain this understanding one has to sit at the feet of the *guru*.

On another occasion in which Svami Karapatriji, Svami Krishnabodha and myself were involved there was a movement related to the slaughter of cows in India. This movement was unique, in all respects, because the *acharyas* of all the sects and divisions of *Sanatana Dharma* from throughout the country, including the Christian and Muslim priests, had assembled there. We were all seated on the platform near the Houses of Parliament, these spiritual dignitaries and religious leaders of the land. Then, the government bribed coolies and policemen started, as if staged beforehand, to set cars on fire, to throw stones and so forth. The police threw tear gas bombs and began to shoot. All the spiritual and religious scholars ran away from the platform except Svami Karapatriji, Svami Krishnabodha and myself. When others asked him to leave the platform I heard Svami Krishnabodha say: "I shall stay here until all others have left; I shall be the last to leave this platform." I said to *Svamiji*, "Those who are worth nothing find their last resort in politics; at present there is not one gentleman in the cabinet and therefore these scoundrels are active". Whereupon he recited the declaration of Arjuna when he entered the battlefield in Kuruskshetra:

"ARJUNASYA PRATIJNAITE NA DAIYAM NA PALAYANAM AYUR RAKSHATI MARMANI AYURANNAM PRAYACCHATI"

"Arjuna assures that no helplessness exists in the battlefield nor desertion. My natural lifespan shall protect the fatal point in my body and that same lifespan will feed me."

After having said this Svami Krishnabodha remained silent for a long time. Sometime later he spoke again. He related how Shri Krishna was about to return from Hastinapura where he had attended an assembly of kings and diplomats to try to mediate for the last time but he failed miserably. In this meeting Shri Krishna called Duryodhana, who had reigned the country for thirteen years, a king of wryness and greed, and promised him that in order to save his own life he would have to walk away from the battlefield, bare-footed and all alone without anyone to help him; and that if this would not so happen Shri Krishna would declare the composers of Dharma as drunkards. *Svamiji* concluded by saying:

"The end of the power of the Congress party has now been inaugurated analogically. This Congress party will never be again what it has been before."

Seeing the present history of India each word of his prediction has become apparent. The party became divided and ultimately almost collapsed: it still holds onto the spokes of the wheel of time which is almost at its end. When *Svamiji* said this to me he was quiet and calm, innermost still with a complete balance of mind and without a trace of anger or motion. When he returned to his *ashram* at last, he was waited upon by many high government functionaries and representatives of the people. After he had drunk a glass of milk they asked him about the next move. He said: "Our task is ended. It is now up to the government and the people". After he has said this he fell quiet and closed his eyes covering his head with a piece of *dhoti*. Under no circumstances did he loose his balance or became wound up; his face did not reflect any reaction. He always remained himself, as a perfect *yogi*. He is a gift to the nation to be proud of: he is the glory of spiritual India.

In Hardvar we attended a very interesting meeting, a *Vedanta* conference which had been organised for the whole of India; it stood under the leadership of Svami Krishnabodha. Karapatriji was the speaker who had asked Svami Krishnabodha to invite me to address the assembly. The meeting had been given more dignity by the presence of *Vedantic* scholars from East and West. Germany, France, America and other countries were represented by excellent speakers. I gave my discourse in English for about forty-five minutes and besides this, I continued for another half hour on request of Svami Krishnabodha. When I had concluded my speech he said to the public that it was a brilliant talk on *Vedanta* and that he had not expected such a masterly treatise of this young *sannyasin*. That talk had brought us close together and since then he cherishes an endless love for me. Only then I understood that he spoke English; he had always kept this a strict secret.

During the same period I met a few other spiritual luminaries of which Svami Maheshvarananda Giri - Mahamandaleshvara was the most celebrated *sannyasin* among *sannyasins*. He is venerated as a jewel among scholars, well versed in all four *Vedas*; the *Upanishads* are at the tip of his tongue, remaining ever surrounded by his disciples - *sannyasins* and householders. A tall figure with brown complexion. Very kind, noble and spiritual. I met him among all the other *sannyasins*. During our talk he understood my Hindi was not fluent and he switched around in the conversation to Sanskrit. Later on we had many private meetings and discussed various spiritual practices.

Svami Akhandananda Sarasvati - Mahamandaleshvara was another spiritual luminary who I met there. He was quiet and calm, moving around, looking after others comforts, avoiding all conflicts and confusion of arguments and debates. He was sitting alone on an unpolished stone, when I met him. Touching his feet I asked him: "May I disturb you?" Then he laughed: "Do you need permission to disturb me? Then you have it." I asked him: "Is it good for us to keep ourselves engaged with these *satsangas* and debates while there are people like you?" He said: "It is necessary - otherwise it will all stop - the tradition of imparting the spiritual knowledge to others. All of you should obtain a proper training of how to maintain the tradition like other traditions. Like a river, small lakes, ponds and streams, one way or the other, directly or indirectly are to join the main river. Otherwise all will become dried up. The fertility of the land will disappear. So is the case with the spiritual tradition and practice. Never miss a chance to speak in *satsanga*. Always be ready with various subjects. Think, discuss it within yourself, refer to the scriptures, be at home, when you get the opportunity to discuss the same with us, then alone you will have the self-confidence and assert yourself as to what you speak is right." This was a great advice for me. I took it into my mind, ever since then I always used to think just after my meditation on various subjects such as the evolution of the cosmic universe, the evolution of the individual human being, plants, sun and moon and so on. I never missed an opportunity to discuss my conclusions on these subjects whenever I met such a spiritual luminary.

Just after this I met Shri Svami Rameshvarananda Giri - Mahamandaleshvara. He is a great scholar in the scriptures and very adept in scriptural discussions and debate. He seldom misses a confrontation. He has the courage, the stamina, skill and technique to put his opponents always in a defensive position. Generally scholars avoid him in confrontation. In his presence he is the central point, who carries away the grammar, grace and victory. He is a master marksman in spiritual and religious debates and discussions. I have learnt some portion of the *Shariraka Bhashya*[1] of Shankaracharya. It was a profitable acquaintance for enriching my spiritual treasure. I always remember him with admiration. He is a slim person. He is very shrewd, clever and often diplomatic.

Mahamandaleshvara means: the lord of a circle of *sannyasins*. Each *mahama* has their own circle of *sannyasin*-disciples consisting of ten to fifteen, twenty to thirty or forty to fifty, in each circle. This group is called a *mandala*. As they are the spiritual preceptor, guide and friend to these *sannyasins* they are called Mahamandaleshvara.

After leaving Hardvar I commenced my solitary sojourn in Northern India. I went to Dehradun. There I spent three days in an *ashram* of the Ramakrishna mission. That *ashram* is meant for the Ramakrishna mission monks to take rest, I was told. It was a nice time for me. The *Svami* was very kind and hospitable. We talked on various

---

1. commentary on the *Brahma-sutras*

subjects amongst ourselves. Then I left to Rajapura, where a *Vedanta* conference is being held under the auspicies of the Shri Svami Ramatirtha mission. Svami Ramatirtha is the most celebrated and illustrious *sannyasin* of Bharat, India. Svami Omkaranandaji is the organiser of the conference. I spent a few days there and gave three talks on the *Vedanta*. Many *sannysins* and *yogins* were present besides thousands of householders.

This occasion I have to mention especially because it was here that I saw, for the first time, among the people, an old *sannyasin* sitting, while bending forward, upwards, pressing his hard buttocks on the ground, adjusting his closed legs in various angles, closing his eyes very hard, shrinking his face, sometimes trying to sit straight, sometimes swinging: I thought he was suffering from a hysterical fit. But on enquiring, I came to know that he was a very big personality: *guru* of one of the Queens of a pappadam state. He is awakening the *Kundalini*. It has become almost his habit to jerk his body and make other gestures to show others the awakening process of the great celebrated *Kundalini*. I was sitting on the speakers platform, when I saw him. Just after the session was over I went to him and paid my respects to him, introducing myself. I came to know that he was educated in England and had been at the bar in his previous *ashram*. During our conversation I noticed that he was very interested in me and he wanted me to remain. I asked him a straight question: "What is this *Kundalini* and why should it be awakened?" He said: "It is a dormant power within all individuals. By awakening it one can attain *samadhi*." Then I asked him: "How such a powerful and mighty force can remain dormant. A force becomes a force, a power becomes a power only when it is expressed, when it makes all the senses and other limbs of the body feel its presence. Even an unshaped diamond makes its presence known by mere shining. If the *Kundalini* is such a mighty power, why does it fail to make its presence known within. Why has it chosen such a place as the coccyx as its abode. Why is such a wonderful power overlooked by all the *Acharayas* and commentators on the *Upanishads* and *Prasthana Traya*?" This question was a surprise and an unexpected intrusion into his intellectual realm. He perceived more arrows, questions that would strike over and over again and that he would be expected to answer.

He kept silent for fifteen minutes and gave a long sigh. Then he said: "It's all a mystery and difficult to answer. Your questions I appreciate. They need time for me to answer. Come tomorrow". I was very anxious to receive his answer, because I too would like to get into that sphere of experience. Pondering over the subject I spent the whole night in trying to understand what type of answer and explanation I would get from this great practitioner of *Kundalini*.

The next morning, just after my meditation and breakfast I made my pilgrimage to him: contrary to my expectation he was surrounded by his disciples. The rich, the educated, the noble and the wise. Some of them were scholars. Introducing me to his disciples he said: "This promising well-educated and qualified *sannyasin* has put to me many wonderful questions about *Kundalini*. Rarely were such questions put by anybody to me so far, though I am seventy-five years old. Then he repeated my questions to them, entire and well. After hearing this, two of his disciples said: "We had those questions too. We would also like to know the answers to these questions." Then the *Svami* asked them: "Why did you not put these questions to me before?" They said: "Because these questions never did strike us so clearly though we had some doubts and because of our fear of you we didn't put these questions. But now, since you yourself have introduced these questions to us we think it is a good time for us to know the answers." Then the *Svami* became silent. He said, breaking his silence after a while: "I was pondering over these questions since he has put them to me. It is all very difficult to answer. You see, the questions and answers are different from knowledge. Experience is knowledge Practice brings experience. Therefore you should practice; then all your doubts will be cleared by yourself. Intellectual discussions do not lead to anything. When you are hungry you have to eat. Talking about eating will not solve your problem.", he concluded.

Immediately I asked him: "Do I first have to practise; before I have heard what it entails, understand what it is and know how to practise? The scriptures say that one first has to listen, then to ponder over it and then meditate upon it. Is this not applicable with the knowledge of the *Kundalini*? I would very much like to practise it under your guidance. You please explain it to me." He smiled, "You are a hard nut to crack", to which I answered, "Knowledge is like a diamond; it radiates its own grace and glow and has its own light and weight. A diamond cannot be cracked like a nut: it has to be kept. The same with knowledge: this has to be illuminated by itself from within. However, to attain knowledge one has to follow a certain definite process. The process is the question: the answer to it is the knowledge." He said, "Very well, let us sing some songs and then leave." I took part in the group singing and when it had finished I touched his feet and took leave. He then asked me, "Are you disappointed?" "No, not at all. I had not tied myself to that knowledge. One has told me that there is no other knowledge than the knowledge of the Self. I follow the process to be able to drink that knowledge drop after drop and obtain them from all directions and many persons, just like a bee." Thereupon he said, "Good."

I thought about my three days stay in Rajapura where there were many *sannyasins*, *sadhus* and scholars present. Except these there were also many great and noble householders, followers of Svami Ramatirtha. Svami Ramatirtha was a great *sannyasin* of the highest realisation. He excelled in detachment as well as realisation. The nineteenth and twentieth century have not produced a *sannyasin* of his calibre with the exception of Ramana Maharishi of this century - my humble prostrations for him.

It was a pleasant situation! A situation which placed us in solitude; surrounded by mountains, free from the noise of civilisation, far from the modern people and free from material life. That spiritual multitude remained in solitude - an ideal place. An ideal place for contemplation! Contemplating on what one heard and what one perceived, on what one perceived and understood. The honest and sincere householders did not know much about *Yoga* but they lived like *yogis* in their traditionally handed down way of life. There was a deep insight and profoundness in their opinions and conduct. They were capable to offer their hard-earned money without attachment; they restrained themselves voluntarily from all comfort and convenience. The householders seemed to me a very great spiritual family, really very great. They did not even know how great they were and that made them humble and noble; that made them still more great. That was the beauty of their lives. Tradition is greater than the knowledge obtained from books. There was a living truth in tradition.

Practice and knowledge from books alone, without tradition, is a useless attempt. Tradition is very great!

A surprising event! An event which did everyone amaze with admiration and surprise. A mother offered her few months old son to the *ashram*. It was astonishing. We could not believe that there could be a mother among householders of such a level of detachment, dedication and devotion. An incident of this kind in human history is very rare. Children may starve and die before their mothers' eyes; they may thieve and murder and become a burden for the family and society, but a mother shall never separate from them, not even involuntarily. This was the only example that I have seen of a mother who offered her dearest child for its spiritual liberation. Even among millions of people, a mother who cares so much for the spiritual liberation and freedom of her child is rare. Detachment, renunciation and devotion to a spiritual purpose are very rare among people in the world, especially when it concerns the question of mother and child. That made this sacrifice such a surprise. Detachment is great when it is derived from knowledge but becomes very painful when it is done mechanically without knowledge.

One day in Rajapura I sat on a rock in silent solitude, far away from the conference, and underwent a new experience. I could see that the inside of my head was illuminated and every blood vessel and nerve was clearly visible. I could see the *Ida* and *Pingala* channels as renowned in *Yoga* but I missed the *Sushumna*. I remained in that state for a long time. It was a balanced state without heat or cold. A state of equilibrium between these two and yet it was light. A revealing light! Because I did not posses much knowledge about the brain, blood vessels and nerves I could not understand much. This experience prompted me to go through a great many texts on *Yoga* and medicine. This strengthened my practice of *hatha yoga* which attained its peak during my stay in Srinagar in Kashmir.

I left Rajapur by bus and went down to Dehradun. From Pathankot to Nurpura, a small village thirteen miles from Pathankot station. I stayed with Mr. Kripal Singh, a retired army officer. On the Monday morning he took me to the village bazaar on the top of the hill. There was a temple, a temple of Shri Krishna. The image of Shri Krishna has a long history. It is said that this statue was worshipped by Mira, a well known devotee of Krishna. Mira was a renowned female saint. She was a queen but did not accept the king as her husband because she had devoted herself to Shri Krishna. She had to undergo many trials and tribulations which formed her into a perfect *Bhakta*, devotee. It has been said that in the last moment she gave up her life merging into this statue. I was told that this statue had been brought from the region of Chittore as a present from its king for the help given to win a battle. The place was quiet and calm, an ideal place for spiritual *sadhana*, sparsely populated and with a dense growth of trees and shrubs, surrounded by large hills and mountains. There stood a very beautiful and old tree in front of the temple and I was told that it was more than three hundred years old. The people living here were very noble, spiritually religious, very simple, kind and merciful.

After my stay of a few days I left for Pathankot. From Pathankot I went by bus to Jammu. This is a town of temples. The town is neat and clean, a typical Hindu town. The people cherish their country and are religious, spiritual, humble and noble; they do not know fear or greed. They are adverse against addictions and bad habits and lead a disciplined and organised life. They protect themselves against disasters and death with courage and religious purity and thus they can be truly called traditional and orthodox people. Most of them belong to the Dogra clan and are very devoted to their family. I have spent two weeks there. I was the guest in the house of one of the leaders of the town. I had met him in the Shiva temple. I do not remember his exact name but he was usually called Sharmaji. He took me to Prema Natha Dogra, also called Panditji. Panditji was tall and strong. He had a robust health and a lean body with intelligent eyes, a large forehead, a prominent nose and a long shaped face that showed spiritual insight. He was an orthodox religious man, convinced and resolute in his actions and visions. He received me with much respect and homage. He was very humble and noble, very friendly and compassionate towards all, irrespective of caste, creed, religion and faith. He was a great politician. After our conversation of an hour I left for the temple where I stayed.

In the Shiva temple I came into contact with many devotees. There were many persons who were truly interested in the practice of *Yoga* and in listening to and knowing *Vedanta*. One of them was a man who had obtained the knowledge of a herb that could change iron into gold but he was not interested in this art. He was satisfied with what he obtained by working hard. He was a poor man and had learned the technique of making gold with the herb from a *yogi*. He put many questions such as, "What is birth? What is death? What is Yoga? What is the Self? What leaves the body and where does it go?" I shall never forget that evening; we kept talking until two o'clock in the morning. They all stayed there to sleep and arose that morning before four o'clock to meditate.

After a few days stay I departed for Shrinagar by bus. It was a pleasant journey with majestic mountains, melodious streams, singing birds, murmuring trees and caressing breezes. But when one looked at the top of the mountain and then to the foot it was frightening. When the bus approached Srinagar the sun - that master artist - had completed its task to not only paint the silver clouds with gold but also the snow-capped mountain peaks, the rivers, the lakes, the trees and the shrubs. The sun was about to withdraw to its abode, to take a bath just like a civilised person, and to take time for meditation. It departed a little earlier as if it did not like to live in the dense darkness and thus gave a chance to the twilight to glow and be admired by the poets and saints.

The bus stopped forty miles before Srinagar, I think in Ramabag, and the next morning at seven o'clock it took us to Srinagar. The ride on the road to Srinagar was very beautiful because the road was straight with Safada trees on both sides which were tall and straight. There were little villages on either side of the road and green land that stretched out to the valleys of the Himalayan mountains; this granted the landscape an unimaginable, majestic beauty.

Srinagar is the summer capital of the state of Jammu and Kashmir. Kashmir has a rich heritage and history and its ancient past is a reservoir of knowledge, of *tantras* and *mantras*. Many *sadhus* of great and high reputation belong to the *Shiva* and *Shakta* sects. There are geniuses in Kashmir who have enriched the *Tantra* literature with their practices and writings of their discoveries concerning worship and supplications. There have been historians, such as Kalhana who is the author of the renowned book *Raja Taramgiri*, a history book about Kashmir and its rulers. Kashmir has also produced scholars like

Abhinava Gupta who was a writer of many commentaries and Eastern texts. Kashmir is full of legends about *tantric* saints and devotees, which keep the whole past alive.

In the middle of Shrinagar is a beautiful hill which is called Shankaracharya hill. It is named after the all-knowing Shankaracharya in memory of his visit to Kashmir. It is said that he has spent his days on this hill in order to fulfil his mission to spread *Vedanta*.

It is inspiring to be in Kashmir. I went there as per invitation of the International Spiritual Parliament that held a conference there, organised by Svami Bhaskarananda. I was lodged in the Abhedananda house - an ashram managed by a *Svamiji* was known as Abhedananda. The Spiritual Parliament was the most amazing forum with which I was ever associated. It was amazing because it was never founded and nobody knows its aim. The organiser had little knowledge about spirituality or the philosophy of *Yoga* and *Vedanta*. But with the organisation as his aim, he had gathered up from here and there, something from the modern writers. The conference was inaugurated by the then present Yuvarani Yasodharadevi. There were many speeches about philosophy and religion. I do not remember at all anything of what was said by any of the speakers, including myself. Whether this was the case because of the debates or because of the manner in which it functioned, I do not know, but it was the only conference that did not impress me. However, I did admire the organisational talent of *Svamiji* to be able to convene such a conference. It is an ability which only few people possess. I do not think this talent is obtained but that it is inborn. Perhaps one is able to develop certain qualities but only on the condition that they are inborn.

After the conference all departed to their respective dwellings. A few *sannyasins* remained there and I was one among them. I came there in contact with a great man called Mr. G.D. Malhotra. He was very noble and generous, kind and compassionate, a man of principle and integrity. He had a large heart, full of love and respect for others. He was cultured and capable. He was a spiritual man though he appeared to have material interests. I was his guest for a few months. He had a wife who was equally great, compassionate, noble and cultured. They had one daughter and two sons - they were all cultured and civilised. When I had a fever, they looked after me as if God had sent them. Because of the severe cold there was snow and I only had some cotton summer-clothes with me, just enough to cover my body. The biting cold activated heat in me, which the doctors called fever. I recovered without any medicines. Through this experience I realised that the heat and cold are one and the same. The dynamics in the human body are amazing and seemingly inexplicable; it produces mind, intelligence and ego all of which originate from the dynamic vibrations producing heat and cold in the body. Heat as well as cold are internal and external. In fact they do not know internal and external, these are the same. It is the mind which perceives heat and cold and makes these to be felt. The human anatomy has no human meaning without the mind, intelligence, ego and, moreover, the soul. The mind which can form and mould a person is wonderful. The mind can even change the functions of the anatomical system in the body. It can make the body vulnerable and invulnerable to heat and cold and all such experiences. If one could control that mind then heat and cold would remain simply as heat and cold but not be able to affect the body. It is the mind which makes us to perceive normally and abnormally.

In fact, it is not only the heat and cold which produce heat and cold. Every object that invokes preference or aversion can produce them. A hot object can produce cold and a cold object can produce heat. There is something dynamic in both; something we perceive, something that changes the nature of the objects; something which changes the object itself - in a certain duration of time. Therefore an object is subject to decay and degeneration - what is progress in fact - it is nothing but the expression of excessive heat which is produced by ones own mind. This is a good word for this. A change is just a change, but when the change is caused by a destructive force or various means one calls it a revolution. In principle revolution is the product of heat. When this is cooled down, we call it peace. This is how the mind works.

Kukkutanaga is a place in Kashmir of interest to tourists. It is a very beautiful place. Awe-inspiring! And tourist inspiring! It has a beautiful waterfall falling from the top of the mountain. It is wonderful to see those mountain peaks belonging to the Himalayan family each having a common tradition from east to west as if marking a borderline of Northern India. There was a beautiful river flowing quiet and calm.

Kukkutanaga was a wonderful place for its quietude and solitude. A less populated virgin land of dense forests. Trees and bushes in abundance cover the major part of the mountain. The melodies of the birds, the comedies of the animals, especially the calves and cows, dogs and cats! Rivulets ever in motion, singing and dancing, flowing! It was the cold season, as in Holland so in Kashmir four months winter and eight months cold. The sun came as a tourist, remaining some time for a few days, a few weeks. They call it summer, but, though the sun used to be there, shining, we needed warm clothes. There were many beautiful springs with, very sweet, rejuvenating water. Kukkutanaga - from the very name one can imagine the position of the landscape, and the mountain, how it appears. Kukkuta means cock. Naga means mountain. Kukkutanaga means "cock-mountain". And so it was shaped too.

The houses - wooden houses. The houses made of wood supported by wooden pillars. There was no ground floor so to say. We had to enter the house up a wooden staircase. There was not much electricity, though it was available there, but not in every house. The progress of electrification went as fast as the walking speed of a paralysed man. I had a hurricane lamp. Being the guest of Mrs. and Mr. Gurudas Malhotra I was provided with several comforts, as if I was a prince.

I had a very important spiritual experience there. One night after meditation as usual I went to bed. I found myself in a state just before deep sleep. A semiconsciousness. I experienced that I was leaving my body. I could see very well how I left my body. *Yogis*, in general, describe the process of giving up the body and entering into another body in a different way. But I found I was going out of the body through a particular nerve in the head. That nerve opened a little. It appeared to me a colour lovely and beautiful, as if painted by a master-artist. Light yellow, light green, and light red. After leaving the body through that, I went, far-off, near to a mountain peak. There I saw a man lying on the ground, just near the river under a tree. I remained near him for some minutes, observing him. He was tall, fair in complexion, with intelligent eyes, a long nose, broad forehead and a well-shaped face; he was lying there as if he was fast asleep. Then someone told me as if from behind: "He is dead. I called you here to teach you how to enter into another's body. You have been cherishing this desire to know how to enter into other's body. So enter into his body." It would be difficult for me to enter, unless I knew the gate of his body. Then suddenly, while I was looking at him I saw the centre of his head open; there was a vein white in colour, pure white. I just entered and I fell fast asleep. My semi-conscious state was no more. I was in deep sleep. Again when I woke up I felt as if I was coming from a distant place. I had a memory of a new experience which I dismissed at once as a dream. Ever since then I was in contemplation on this event. I couldn't understand how this experience came about. I know that dreams are the impressions of the wakeful state come in the form of memory, awakened in the subtle body, before one gets into deep sleep in the causal body. But this I had never experienced before, at least I feel I don't have a right to experience it. It is meant for *yogis* of a higher calibre, I thought. If I had had this knowledge in the past, in my previous birth, I would not have been here in this stage. I could not make out what it was. I am sure I was not sleeping at that time. I have told this story to my disciples, Mrs.Susheela Malhotra and to her husband Mr. Gurudas Malhotra next morning itself, probably during our breakfast. I try to forget this experience as meaningless, purposeless, but it remains within me. This memory ever comes in solitude as a sweet memory of a pleasant incident. Since then I was very interested to meet the *yogis* of name and fame. The *yogis* who are famous among *sannyasins* of serious and honest nature. But, ever since then I have a feeling that I had a fall from my path towards *Samadhi*. The metempsychosis is very much inferior to *Samadhi*. All my practices were meant to lead me to *Samadhi*. Yet of course, as I had heard of these abilities, and learned some things to certain extent from great *yogis*, I had been cherishing an aspiration to experience the feat of metempsychosis.

Returning to Srinagar I heard a story from Mrs.Malhotra. A lady who was dead came back again to her body before it was burned. She had experienced walking on sharp stones and thorns, the pains and pangs of the departure from her body and of the life that she spent before she came back to her own body, as she herself stated. This was a story of great interest for me.

Mrs. Malhotra told me of another incident of a lady with her husband and relatives who while going up Shankaracarya Hill near

Srinagar, was about to reach the top, then she felt tired and sat down. She saw three veins in her head, clearly, full of light. She talked about this to the others including her husband and she said; "I am going to give up my body", and thus she passed away. How this lady could have this vision of these veins, the *Ida* and *Pingala* and *Sushumna*.

Is it possible to see them at all for an ordinary person, who did not undergo the disciplines of *Yoga*? An amazing incident. Perhaps, there are many amusing and amazing wonderful incidents in human life. Within the human constitution, within its living mechanism, the whole universe is said to exist.

As many accidents and incidents take place, unconsciously, in the wakeful state, so it is possible within everyone. For incidents and accidents do not need any process known to us. They have their own cause and method to appear and disappear. It is very difficult to analyse. Yet, it is not reasonable or fair just to dismiss them altogether, as modern scholars do with whatever they cannot understand, as a myth or as mystic nonsense. That needs a super blindness. Nothing can happen without a definite process, whether it is visual illusion or mental projection.

One evening I went to sleep as usual, just four or five minutes after closing my eyes I saw a white light, a cooling light, a pleasant light, just above me on the ceiling of my room and square in shape. It was so peaceful to see. I saw it again and again many times, even during my siesta. I opened my eyes to look at it and wondered what it was. Then it vanished. This kind of experience I used to have often during my worship. It is very difficult to have a rational explanation for it. The event is easy to explain, and it could be dismissed as a visual illusion. But what we call experience is something beyond visualisation and reason. In fact, a right experience is knowledge itself. Knowledge cannot be reasoned, as the knowledge itself is the basis for reason. We reason in the light of knowledge. Even when we reason, we are not reasoning knowledge - the experience, but the process how, and not the experience itself. Seldom one is capable of knowing the process of their experience which happens unconsciously, almost by accident.

When the experience is the result of an experiment, then it is very clear and easy to explain. When it is by chance, then one is at a loss to find a way to explain it; but my knowledge of psychology and philosophy do not admit an accident or a chance incident. That kept me continuously, wondering about the subject, pondering on the topic.

Kashmir - I used to visit it almost every winter for six years from 1955 onwards. These were some of the best years of my best life. By the best life I mean the period of my life in which I used to learn and practice *Yoga* and *Vedanta*, meeting with *sannyasins* and visit *ashrams* and good families of spiritual and divine glamour. That part of life laid down a strong foundation for my future spiritual practices, experiences and expressions. There is nothing greater than coming into contact with great men - like *sannyasins*. *Sannyasins* in general are great - and some in particular greater still. To be with them, to listen to them, to look at them and to feel their presence is elevating, sublimating one into a different realm of life. Though *sannyasins* are also human beings, their time, space and causation greatly differ from others. Hence, people in general do not understand them. Spiritual luminaries are not ruled by the solar system or lunar system either. They are ruled by a system which is spiritual and divine. It is natural to them to live according to scriptures and strictures. The period of my life which I spent amongst them is what I call the best part of my life. Alone in multitude. It is only amongst their presence that I felt no identification, but felt emancipation. *Sannyasins* are very great. The moment one takes them as an ordinary human being like the government does, or as political imposters do by attiring in their garments, they remain closed within themselves and appear as ordinary human beings. What makes a human being a *sannyasin* is not seen or understood by the government or political agents. Therefore, the *sannyasins* very often become victims to these special human bodies and the constitutional mechanism, which is called government. My every visit to Kashmir enriched me with spiritual practices and experiences. During this period of six years I did not give any spiritual discourses nor was I interested to discuss much either, but I was extremely interested to listen.

Listening is a great elevating process. Listening gives a better chance to learn. While listening alone one can attain wisdom. Talking needs study; even for gossip one needs a vast study on various subjects. It is a sin to become a chatterbox or a talkative fellow.

Persons who are fond of talking, they always talk about others, definitely not good things about others, but about other's shortcomings, faults, omissions. If there is no one to talk of, they will project someone and talk in the same way. They split their mind, they create doubts and confusion in the minds of others about any person. It is a dangerous habit. But many people patronise this habit. In listening to others one can eliminate completely these habits and get out of identification.

I left the Himalayas meditating upon my experiences and of what I heard from others; even to think of them was a very happy thing.

OM

A Solitary traveller

GLOSSARY

acharya Learned teacher, usually a respected Sannyasin.

antahkarana chatushtaya The inner organ consisting of four functions: the mind, ego, memory and intelligence.

ardha Half.

asura Wicked demi-gods, non-gods.

ayurveda Indian medicine, literally the science of life

ayurvedic concerning ayurveda.

Bhagavad Gita Philosophical treatise on dharma, presented in poetical verses, as a dialogue between Arjuna and Lord Shri Krishna. Part of the epic The Mahabharata.

Bhagavatpada India's greatest saint-philosopher who revived the Vedanta by writing commentaries on the most important texts and by spreading its knowledge among the people of India; Pujya - revered.

bhakta A spiritually devoted person.

bharata India.

bharitiya rashtriyata Indian Nationhood.

bhashya Commentary.

bhiksha Alms; brahmins, brahmacharis or sannyasins requesting alms from householders, as their righteous duty or dharma, when they go to five houses in the morning after 11 a.m., requesting a handful of food from each house.

Brahman The Absolute existence-knowledge-bliss.

Brahma-puri lit. The city of Brahman, the space in the heart of the head.

brahmana A person in whom sattvaguna prevails.

brahmin A brahmana, in whom sattvaguna prevails

caturmasi Four months' stay at one place.

Charaka Author of an authoritative text on Ayurveda.

Citishakti The power of the Self-luminous Self.

citta The store-house of impressions, the memory.

C-trinity Concentration, contemplation, culmination. see Samyama.

Daksha King of Kankhal; father of Sati.

darshana Philosophy; point of view; school of thought.

deva A demi-god.

dharma Substratum; the fundamental code of conduct; righteousness.

Gangotri The source of the river Ganga.

Ganga The river Ganges.

Girija Another name of Parvati, the wife of Lord Shiva.

Gita Song, common name for Bhagavad Gita.

grihastha A householder; period between student life and old age, when a family is raised and householders duties are performed.

guna Force of manifestation of which there are three: rajoguna, tamoguna and sattvaguna

guru Spiritual preceptor.

Gurudev Reverent title for one's guru.

Hara The destroyer of all afflictions and modifications.

Hardvar A holy town at the foot of the Himalayas; meditating from where one can realise the Hara, the destroyer of modifications and afflictions.

Hastinapura The capital of the kingdom of Duryodhana.

hatha-yoga The science of controlling the body and purifying the internal system of the body.

Himavan The mountain range named the Himalayas.

Himavat The mountains of the Himalayas.

Hrdaya The heart of the head.

hrdayakasa The space in the heart of the head.

Hrishikesh One of the holy towns in the Himalayan region, North of Hardvar; the lord of the senses

ida One of the three nadis (subtle nerves) in the head, generating coolness.

indu Moon, (drop in the sky); drop.

itihasa Thus it happened.

jnana Knowledge

jnana-yogi The competent yogi who practices yoga only through knowledge, not through actions.

Jyeshtha A goddess, lit. the eldest.

Kailasa Mountain in the Northern Himalayas on which Shiva used to meditates (abode of Lord Shiva).

kali Black.

Kalidasa Renowned Indian poet and dramatist.

kalikambli Black woollen blanket.

kalikamblivala Wearing a black blanket.

Kalikamblivala sattram A place where one can stay free of cost.

kamandalu Waterpot which sannyasins carry on their journey.

Kankhal A town, the capital city of Daksha.

karma Action; sometimes actions and their results.

karma-yogi The yogi who performs actions by surrendering their
   motivations and results to the Ishvara, to God.

kumbha A pot.

kumbhamela A great gathering of saints once in twelve years.

kundalini Dormant power according to rajayoga.

maha Great.

Mahalakshmi The goddess of prosperity health and happiness.

Mahamandaleshvara The chief guru of a group of sannyasins.

Mahameru Mountain used in the process of the churning of the
   ocean.

maharishi A great seer, saint and wise man.

mala A rosary for japa - the repetition of the mantra.

mandala A circle; a group of persons.

mandika Temple.

mandira Temple.

manana The second of a three part process to self-realisation where
   one reflects, ponders and solves any doubts about the subjects
   heard; lit. thinking.

mantra Sacred sound power; lit. protector of the mind.

mela Fair, large gathering.

mudra Technique of the Hatha-yoga which purifies the internal
   systems of the body and which awakens happiness.

nididhyasana The third of a three part process to self-realisation
   where one meditates on the subjects heard and reflected upon.

Om Sacred syllable which leads one to Ishvara, God.

pingala One of the three nadis (or veins) generating heat.

Prajapati The protector of all beings.

prajna Culminante intelligence.

Pranava Which leads to the Ishvara, the Om.

Pranayama The control of the bio-energic force. A means to control
   the mind.

prarabdha The result of actions, good or bad, performed in the past.

pratyahara Introspective state in which the senses and the mind are withdrawn.

prasamkyana samadhi The discrimination between the self and the non self - vivekakhyati.

prasthana traya The three basic texts of Vedanta: the Upanishads, the Bhagavad Gita, the Brahma-sutras.

rajoguna The force of motion and projection.

rishi Seer; saint.

sadhu A practitioner of restraints in order to attain perfection.

sadguru Spiritual preceptor guiding others to the "sat", the self; the highest guru.

sadhana Practise of the methods leading to spiritual enlightenment.

sadhana-chatushtaya The four fold practices of viveka (discrimination), vairagya (detachment), shatsampatti (the six-fold such as shama and dama), mumukshutva (desire for liberation).

sahasra-padmam A thousand petaled lotus which denotes the brain.

samadhi Culmination of meditation.

samadhi-prajna The culminant intelligence established in culmination.

samapatti The culmination practised as part of the yoga process.

samvid-hrdayam Synonym of hrdayakasha, the place to meditate in the head.

samyama the practise of concentration, contemplation and culmination together.

Sanatana Dharma Also called Hindu dharma; sanatana - eternal; dharma - the substratal code of conduct.

sannyasa Renunciation from the world.

sannyasin A renunciant.

Sanskrit The ancient Indian language in which all text concerning Sanatana Dharma and concerning the self have been expounded.

sarasvati One of the ten orders of sannyasins.

Sati Name of Parvati in her previous birth.

satsanga Spiritual discourse.

sattram Place where free accommodation and food is given to sannyasins and others.

sattvaguna The force of equilibrium.

Shankara Name for Bhagavadpada.

Shankaracharya lit. The teacher Shankara.

shatsampatti The six restraints of shama, dama, uparati, titiksha,shraddha and samadhana.

shikha A tuft of hair which brahmins wear covering the hrdayakasha.

shirohrdayam lit. The heart of the head.

shravana The first of a three part process to self realisation where one listens only and with concentration to subjects related to self.

sthita-prajna A yogi who is established in Brahman, as explained in the Bhagawad Gita.

sushumna The subtlest and shortest nadi (nerve) in the head which runs from the hrdayakasha up to the crown of the head.

Sushruta Author of an authoritative text on Ayurveda.

svami One who is master over oneself.

svamiji A respectful title for a svami.

tamoguna The force of inertia (lethargy), the veiling force.

Upanishads The text of Vedanta forming the last part of the Vedas.

vana Forest or knowledge.

veda lit. Knowledge; the ancient scriptures of Sanatana Dharma.

Vedanta In which all knowledge culminates; the philosophy of the oneness of the soul and brahman.

Vedantasara lit. The essence of Vedanta; title of a text written by Sadananda Yogindra.

Vedantic Pertaining to Vedanta.

vina Classical stringed instrument.

vyutthana Awakened state of impressions.

Yoga The process and the state of yoga that is the prevention of all modifications of the mind.

Yoga-sutra The text on yoga written by Maharishi Patanjali.

yogangas The path of the process of yoga named yama, niyama, asana, pranayama, pratyahara, dharana, dhyana and samadhi.

Yoga-Vasishtha A classical text on yoga.

yogi One who is established in the state of yoga or who practises the yogangas with the direct aim to attain the state of yoga.

yogic Related to yoga.

Luminary Publications of the
Universal Confluence of Yoga-Vendānta Luminary

Luminary Publications publishes all works of Svāmi Sadānanda Sarasvatī and other qualified literature relevant to Yoga and Vedānta philosophy, in the form of books and booklets, magazines and journals, leaflets and pamphlets.

Svāmi Sadānanda Sarasvatī was the founder of the Universal Confluence of Yoga-Vedānta Luminary (UCYL) which, since 1972, facilitates and propagates the teachings of Yoga and Vedānta and its practical application in the daily life of people.

The UCYL aims to uplift spiritual values; promote peace, health and harmony; teach methods of correct perception and to engender an understanding of how to face problems in daily life. UCYL also aims at illuminating the path of Self-realisation and has therefore founded Āshrams and Yoga centres in Wales, The Netherlands, France and India.

In 1981 the UCYL was established in Great Britain where it holds regular Haṭhayoga, Yoga and Vedānta classes, group discussions, children's programmes and study weekends.

For further information please contact:
Luminary Publications
Ābhedashram, Marcella, Salop Road,
Welshpool, Powys SY21 7ET Great Britain.
Tel: 01938 554068
International Tel: +44 1938 554068

Some Other Works by
Svāmi Sadānanda Sarasvatī

Reflections

Words of wisdom on a variety of topics extracted from the satsangas
of Svāmiji over a number of years. Full of wit, humour and profound
philosophical insight.

ISBN 0 950522 0 2   Price: £4.95

Yogānuśāsānam

Commentary on the "Yogasutras" of Patanjali.

Vedāntasāra

Commentary on the "Vedāntasāra" (essence of Vedānta) of
Sadānanda Yogīndra.

Haṭhayoga: Theory and Practice

Systematic explanations of the most important Haṭhayoga postures,
mudrās and prāṇāyāmas.

These titles are available from Luminary Publications

Printed by Business Colour Ltd., Henfaes Lane, Welshpool, Powys SY21 7BE, UK